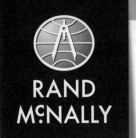

W9-BKK-187

2022

Road Atlas

Contents

Travel Information

National Parks ii–xiii
America's national parks inspire wonder and awe, restore our souls, and renew our faith in the nation. Rand McNally presents "The National Parks by Decade," a review of the national parks and their status through the decades.

Tourism Contacts xiv
Phone numbers and websites for tourism information in each state and province.

Road Construction and Road Conditions Resources xv
Numbers to call and websites to visit for road information in each state and province.

Hotel Resources 81

Mileage Chart 82
Driving distances between 77 North American cities.

Mileage and Driving Times Map inside back cover
Distances and driving times between over a hundred North American cities.

Maps

Map legend inside front cover

United States overview map 2–3

U.S. states 4–53

Canada overview map 54–55

Canadian provinces 56–63

Mexico overview map and Puerto Rico 64

U.S. and Canadian cities 65–80

Published and printed in U.S.A.

For licensing information and copyright permissions, contact us at permissions@randmcnally.com

If you have a comment, suggestion, or even a compliment, please visit us at randmcnally.com/tellrand
or write to:
Rand McNally Consumer Affairs
P.O. Box 7600
Chicago, Illinois 60680-9915

State & Province Maps

United States
Alabama	4
Alaska	5
Arizona	6
Arkansas	7
California	8-9
Colorado	12
Connecticut	10-11
Delaware	13
Florida	14
Georgia	15
Hawaii	5
Idaho	16
Illinois	17
Indiana	18
Iowa	19
Kansas	22
Kentucky	20-21
Louisiana	23
Maine	24
Maryland	13
Massachusetts	10-11
Michigan	25
Minnesota	26
Mississippi	27
Missouri	28
Montana	29
Nebraska	30
Nevada	8-9
New Hampshire	31
New Jersey	32
New Mexico	33
New York	34-35
North Carolina	36-37
North Dakota	38
Ohio	40-41
Oklahoma	42
Oregon	43
Pennsylvania	44-45
Rhode Island	10-11
South Carolina	36-37
South Dakota	39
Tennessee	20-21
Texas	46-47
Utah	50
Vermont	31
Virginia	48-49
Washington	51
West Virginia	48-49
Wisconsin	52
Wyoming	53

Canada
Alberta	57
British Columbia	56
Manitoba	59
New Brunswick	63
Newfoundland and Labrador	63
Nova Scotia	63
Ontario	60-61
Prince Edward Island	63
Québec	62
Saskatchewan	58

City Maps
Albuquerque	65
Atlanta	65
Austin	66
Baltimore	65
Birmingham	65
Boston	66
Buffalo	67
Charlotte	66
Chicago	67
Cincinnati	68
Cleveland	69
Columbus	68
Dallas	69
Denver	68
Detroit	70
Fort Lauderdale	72
Fort Worth	69
Greensboro	70
Hartford	69
Houston	71
Indianapolis	70
Jacksonville	69
Kansas City	72
Las Vegas	72
Los Angeles	73
Louisville	70
Memphis	74
Mexico City	64
Miami	72
Milwaukee	74
Minneapolis	71
Nashville	73
New Orleans	74
New York	75
Newark	75
Norfolk	74
Orlando	77
Ottawa	55
Philadelphia	76
Phoenix	74
Pittsburgh	77
Portland	76
Raleigh	78
St. Louis	76
St. Paul	71
St. Petersburg	78
Sacramento	78
Salt Lake City	79
San Antonio	78
San Diego	78
San Francisco	79
Seattle	77
Tampa	78
Toronto	80
Vancouver	80
Washington D.C.	80
Winston-Salem	70

RAND McNALLY

The National Parks by Decade

More Than a Century of America the Beautiful

America's national parks inspire wonder and awe, restore our souls, and renew our faith in the nation. The sight of steaming volcanoes, rushing rivers, snowcapped peaks, vibrant coral reefs, shimmering deserts, and lush forests reminds us of America's amazing spirit and its astonishing beauty.

Since its founding in 1916, the National Park Service (NPS) has served as the official caretaker of many wondrous sites, first among them, the parks themselves. Some were previously protected under different designations: Hot Springs in Arkansas, for example, was first set aside as a "federal reservation for future recreation" (back in 1832!), and many a site was originally a national monument (NM). Through the years, parks have also been reconfigured, enlarged through land purchases, or renamed. Here is a rundown of the national parks and their status through the decades.

Above, (clockwise from top left): Island fox, Channel Islands National Park; Indiana Dunes National Park; Glacier Bay National Park and Preserve; Shenandoah National Park; Kayaking, Big Bend National Park; Toroweap Overlook, North Rim, Grand Canyon National Park; Crater Lake National Park; Cliff Palace, Mesa Verde National Park.

Early Years (Late-1800s–1900s)

The Yosemite and Yellowstone Story

How did it all begin? Although the NPS wasn't formally established until August 25, 1916, its origins can be traced to the 1860s, when citizens—astounded by the majesty of a remote California valley—managed to advance a bill through Congress. After receiving the bill and seeing the accompanying images of the valley, President Abraham Lincoln agreed that this land should be protected from development. He signed the Yosemite Grant Act on June 30, 1864, and though Yosemite wouldn't be designated a national park until 1890, this act set a precedent.

Eight years later, word of bubbling earth, spouts of steam, and trees of stone reached Washington. The result? In 1872, Yellowstone became a national park—the country's first site to be designated as such.

Other Inductees: Sequoia, CA (1890). Mount Rainier, WA (1899). Crater Lake, OR (1902). Wind Cave, SD (1903). Mesa Verde, CO (1906).

View of El Capitan and Half Dome formations, Yosemite National Park, CA.

1910s

Grand Canyon National Park, AZ (1919)

It was established as a NM in 1908, and by the time it was made a park 11 years later, the Grand Canyon—with its unreal dimensions (1-mile deep, 18-miles wide, and 277-miles long) and ever-changing kaleidoscope of colors—had become iconic. Contemplate its beauty by gazing out from a quiet spot along the rim, by hiking down into it a short distance, or by trekking all the way to its floor—on foot or by mule. Alternatively, observe the canyon from the sky via helicopter or plane, or embark on a hair-raising Colorado River white-water rafting expedition. Regardless of how you choose to see it . . . see it!

Other Inductees: Glacier, MT (1910). Rocky Mountain, CO (1915). Haleakalā and Hawai'i Volcanoes, HI (1916, both as part of Hawaii NP; names changed in 1960 and 1961, respectively). Lassen Volcanic, CA (1916; originally Cinder Cone and Lassen Peak NMs 1907). Denali, AK (1917 as Mt. McKinley; name changed in 1980). Acadia, ME (1919 as Lafayette NP, with a name change in 1929; originally Sieur de Monts NM 1916). Zion, UT (1919; originally Mukuntuweap NM 1909).

Old Faithful geyser, Yellowstone National Park, WY (above).

The Narrows, Zion National Park, UT (left).

Parks 101

The NPS oversees more than 400 units that include not only parks, but also preserves, monuments, lakeshores, seashores, recreation areas, scenic rivers and trails, memorials, parkways, battlefields, and historic parks and sites. In addition, the NPS plays an advisory role for the more than 50 National Heritage Areas: regions and/or communities whose landscapes, structures, trails, and byways have earned a chapter in the American story. All of this is yours to discover.

NATIONAL PARKS

Learn Something New

Many parks have amazing (and often free) ranger-led tours and other programs. Institutes and field schools offer courses on a vast array of topics from astronomy, biology, botany, and conservation to photography, storytelling, art, crafts, music, yoga—even mountaineering and survival skills.

Take a Pass

Several cost-saving America the Beautiful passes make your national parks even more accessible. The recommended **Annual Pass**, available to everyone, offers admission to national parks and other federal lands for 12 months from date of purchase. Note, too, that this pass is available free to active-duty military personnel and their dependents.

To introduce youngsters to the parks (as well as to national forests, marine sanctuaries, and wildlife refuges), the **Every Kid Outdoors Pass** offers free entry to fourth graders—and their family members and friends—for the duration of the school year.

The **Annual Senior Pass**, available for a nominal fee, and the **Lifetime Senior Pass** are options for U.S. citizens or permanent residents age 62 and up. The **Access Pass** is free to U.S. citizens or permanent residents with permanent disabilities, and the **Volunteer Pass** costs nothing for those with 250 service hours at federal agencies participating in the Interagency Pass Program.

Part-Time Park Time?

Enroll in the **Volunteers-in-Parks** (www.nps.gov/getinvolved/volunteer.htm) program, and you'll join over 279,000 dedicated souls who work side-by-side with about 20,000 NPS employees. In addition, many official park concessionaires hire paid part- or full-time employees to work in hotels, restaurants, and gift shops.

Check **USAjobs.gov**, the federal government's official employment site, or the **national park site**, which has sections on **jobs/careers** (www.nps.gov/aboutus/workwithus.htm) and a searchable list of **authorized concessionaires** (www.nps.gov/subjects/concessions/authorized-concessioners.htm).

You can also check out the websites of several large private companies that manage select park-based hotels, restaurants, and stores. These include **Aramark** (www.aramark.com), **Delaware North** (www.delawarenorth.com), and **Xanterra** (www.xanterra.com).

The Contact List

National Heritage Areas: www.nps.gov/heritageareas or www.nationalheritageareas.us
National Park Service: www.nps.gov
National Park Foundation: www.nationalparks.org
National Parks Conservation Association: www.npca.org
Recreation.gov: 877/444-6777, www.recreation.gov; trip-planning assistance, park campground reservations, attraction and event tickets

1920s

Grand Teton National Park, WY (1929)

The heroic dimensions of the wide-open West will command your attention, but your eyes will likely settle on the massive row of mountains whose image doubles in mirror-like Jackson Lake. Early French-Canadian trappers called this mountain range Les Trois Tetons (The Three Breasts), with Grand Teton being the most prominent. Most lodgings here offer incredible views. And between Yellowstone (roughly 60 miles north) and Jackson (about 30 miles south), you'll experience a dash of excitement when negotiating the alpine-like curves of the John D. Rockefeller Jr. Memorial Parkway.

Other Inductees: Hot Springs, AR (1921; change from 1832 status as a "federal reservation"). Bryce Canyon, UT (1928; NM 1908).

Bison in Grand Teton National Park, WY.

1930s

Great Smoky Mountains National Park, NC/TN (1934)

Well and firmly established for development as a national park by 1934 (though not formally dedicated as such until 1940), Great Smoky Mountains has a backstory that embodies the spirit of the decade. In the 1920s, after unrestrained logging had devastated the region, a unique confederation of private citizens—from schoolchildren to philanthropists like John D. Rockefeller Jr.—and local, state, and federal governments united to purchase some 800 square miles of property. In the 1930s, the Civilian Conservation Corps (CCC) went to work replanting forests, restoring old buildings, and creating park infrastructure.

Today, when you travel US Highway 441 across the Smoky Mountains, you'll see wetlands; grassy balds; waterfalls; a greater variety of trees than exists in all of Europe; and sights such as Cades Cove, where a community of mountain families once lived. Visit between late May and mid-June, and you might catch a nighttime performance of synchronous fireflies—nature at its choreographed best.

Other Inductees: Carlsbad Caverns, NM (1930; NM 1923). Everglades (1934, though not dedicated until 1947). Shenandoah, VA (1935). Olympic, WA (1938; originally Mt. Olympus NM 1909).

Formations in the Big Room, Carlsbad Caverns National Park.

Rialto Beach, Olympic National Park, WA.

Roaring Fork, Great Smoky Mountains National Park, TN.

POPULARITY CONTEST

Filmmaker Ken Burns' observation that national parks are "America's best idea" seems borne out by their popularity. On average, combined visitation to all the parks and other NPS sites—across every state, the District of Columbia, and several territories—is more than 320 million people annually. Here are the five most-visited national parks:

Great Smoky Mountains, NC/TN: 12.5 million

Grand Canyon, AZ: More than 5.97 million

Rocky Mountain, CO: 4.7 million

Zion, UT: 4.5 million

Yosemite, CA: 4.4 million

1940s

Big Bend National Park, TX (1944)

Everything is big in Texas, including this 801,163-acre park on the Texas–Mexico border, where much of the landscape was an ancient seabed that now conceals dinosaur bones and other fossils. Canyons cut into the limestone rock and leather-like desert, where only the toughest wildlife thrives and only the hardiest vegetation blooms. Still, throughout its history, six nations claimed ownership of this rugged, inhospitable land; Native Americans, Spanish explorers, and hardscrabble pioneers inhabited it over the centuries.

Here, too, it's not just what surrounds you that will amaze. It's also what's above. Big Bend is a certified International Dark Sky Park, which means that its coal-black nighttime sky truly showcases all those stars.

Other Inductees: Isle Royale, MI (1940). Kings Canyon, CA (1940). Mammoth Cave, KY (1941).

Mule Ears formation, Big Bend National Park, TX.

1950s

Virgin Islands National Park, USVI (1956)

More than half of the island of St. John and most of neighboring Hassel Island is national parkland. What does this mean for your Caribbean vacation? Well, you can hike through paradise on your pick of more than 20 beachside and backcountry trails, discovering salt ponds, waterfalls, rain forests, historic ruins, and ancient petroglyphs. And that's only part of it. Much of the park is underwater, so you can snorkel or dive amid seagrass beds, coral reefs, and colorful marine life. And there's no better place to do absolutely nothing than on the white sands of Trunk Bay, consistently named one of the world's best beaches.

Other Inductees: So, here's a bit of trivia for you—Virgin Islands was the only park inductee of the decade!

Trunk Bay, Virgin Islands National Park, U.S. Virgin Islands.

Saguaro National Park, AZ.

IN THEIR OWN LEAGUE

When ranked by size, Alaska's parks own the top five spots:

Wrangell-St. Elias: 13.2 million acres

Gates of the Arctic: 8.3 million acres

Denali: 6.1 million acres

Katmai: 4.1 million acres

Lake Clark: 4.0 million acres

Autumnal landscape in
Denali National Park, AK.

1960s

North Cascades National Park, WA (1968)

How do you know you're standing above a collision of tectonic plates? Well, you'll see peaks that rise more than 9,000 feet and valleys that plunge to a few hundred feet above sea level. North Cascades is as diverse as it is dramatic. West of the Cascade Crest is a temperate rain forest; to the east, an ecosystem of dry ponderosa pine. This is a world of wetlands and evergreens, of alpine wilderness and glaciers, of 300 lakes and ponds, and of more than 1,600 identified (so far) plant species.

Winter climbing, North Cascades
National Park, WA.

Other Inductees: Petrified Forest, AZ (1962; NM 1906). Canyonlands, UT (1964). Redwood, CA (1968).

Wrangell-St. Elias National Park & Preserve, AK.

Channel Islands National Park, CA.

1970s

Voyageurs National Park, MN (1975)

"Voyageurs" is French for "travelers," a none-too-subtle hint that this park—with its calm lakes; rugged shorelines; and woods of spruce, fir, aspen, birch, pine, and oak—is definitely worth exploring. The proliferation of interconnected waterways makes fishing, boating, and guided canoe trips along historic trading routes popular pastimes. Should you desire "luxury," you can rent a houseboat. In this hardy environment, outdoor activities don't stop when it's cold; there's snowmobiling, snowshoeing, sledding, and ice fishing. It's likewise delightful at night. Here in the North Country, you might be treated to the otherworldly glow of the aurora borealis.

Other Inductees: Arches, UT (1971; NM 1929). Capitol Reef, UT (1971; NM 1937). Guadalupe Mountains, TX (1972). Badlands, SD (1978; NM 1929). Theodore Roosevelt, ND (1978; originally National Memorial Park 1947).

1980s

Wrangell-St. Elias National Park & Preserve, AK (1980)

Four mountain ranges converge in this park, which truly is a place of superlatives. It has 9 of America's 16 highest peaks, including 18,009-foot Mount St. Elias; North America's largest piedmont glacier, the Malaspina, which is up to 2,000 feet thick and larger than the state of Rhode Island; and massive Mount Wrangell, one of North America's largest volcanoes, which last erupted in 1884–85. The wildlife (caribou,

moose, migratory birds, sea lions, harbor seals) makes this park even more magnificent. And it's huge: as big as Yellowstone, Yosemite, and Switzerland combined!

Other Inductees: Biscayne, FL (1980; NM 1968). Channel Islands, CA (1980; NM 1938). Gates of the Arctic, Glacier Bay, Katmai, Kenai Fjords, Kobuk Valley, and Lake Clark—all in AK (1980; all were previously NMs). Great Basin, NV (1986; originally Lehman Caves NM 1922). American Samoa (1988; though land wasn't officially available to the NPS until 1993).

1990s

Fort Jefferson, Dry Tortugas National Park, FL.

Dry Tortugas National Park, FL (1992)

Although Key West is as far south as you can go in the Lower 48, some travelers don't think that's going far enough. They head 70 miles west of Key West to this 100-square-mile park at the confluence of the Gulf of Mexico and the Atlantic Ocean. Most of the park is open water, which accentuates its seven keys—Garden, Loggerhead, Bush, Long, East, Hospital, and Middle—collectively known as the Dry Tortugas. Its focal point, though, is the mid-1800s Fort Jefferson, the largest all-masonry fort in the United States. Visitors arrive via boat or seaplane to explore the fortress, which was made a NM in 1935, and dive amid coral reefs and shipwrecks.

Other Inductees: Death Valley, CA/NV (1994; NM 1933). Joshua Tree, CA (1994; NM 1936). Saguaro, AZ (1994; NM 1933). Black Canyon of the Gunnison, CO (1999; NM 1933).

Canoeing on Swiftcurrent Lake in Glacier National Park, MT.

BIG-TIME LOWER 48

The five largest parks in the continental United States give you land . . . lots of land!

Death Valley, CA/NV: 3.4 million acres

Yellowstone, ID/MT/WY: 2.2 million acres

Everglades, FL: 1.5 million acres

Grand Canyon, AZ: 1.2 million acres

Glacier, MT: 1.0 million acres

2000s

Cuyahoga Valley National Park, OH (2000)

Midway between Cleveland and Akron, this 33,000-acre park, previously established (1974) as a National Recreation Area, captures the quiet appeal of America's Heartland. It follows the flow of the Cuyahoga River, whose banks are bordered by deep forests, rolling hills, and open farmland. You can walk, run, or bike along the Towpath Trail, which follows the historic route of the Ohio & Erie Canal. Other highlights include Beaver Marsh, a wetland accessible via a boardwalk; the 19th-century Everett Covered Bridge; the Canal Exploration Center; the canal-side 1836 Boston Store, which is now the visitors center; the 1.5-mile Brandywine Gorge Trail; and the 65-foot-high Brandywine Falls.

Other Inductees: Congaree, SC (2003; NM 1976). Great Sand Dunes, CO (2004; NM 1932).

The scenery at sunset in White Sands National Park, NM (above).

Rock climbing in Pinnacles National Park, CA (below).

Brandywine Falls, Cuyahoga Valley National Park, OH.

2010s

White Sands National Park, NM (2019)

How white (and fine) are the sands at this, the decade's last site to achieve national park status? Well, as you motor along the scenic Dunes Drive, squint your eyes (and turn up the air-conditioning!), and you might believe you're in a winter wonderland. Hike one of the trails, though, and there's no doubt you're in the northern Chihuahuan Desert. Ironically, you can enjoy what is normally a cold-weather pursuit amid the heat: sledding down the powdery mounds, some as high as 60 feet, is a very popular activity here.

The world's largest gypsum dune field is the byproduct of ancient geologic history. The surrounding area is the byproduct of modern history: the Atomic Age was ushered in at the U.S. Army's nearby missile range, where the first atomic bomb was tested—and other projectiles still are.

Other Inductees: Pinnacles, CA (2013; NM 1908). Gateway Arch, MO (2018; originally Jefferson National Expansion Memorial 1935). Indiana Dunes, IN (2019; originally National Lakeshore 1966).

2020s

New River Gorge National Park & Preserve, WV (2020)

Designated a National River in 1978, New River Gorge became the first national park of the decade in late December of 2020. West Virginia's sole national park spans over 70,000 acres along 53 miles of the New River and is noted for top-notch hiking, whitewater rafting, rock climbing, and fishing. Home to the deepest river gorge in the Appalachian Mountains, New River has a substantial ecosystem that includes unique varieties of indigenous fish, as well as diverse species of mammals, birds, reptiles, and plants.

New River Gorge Bridge in New River Gorge National Park & Preserve, WV (right).

Scenic overview, Isle Royale National Park, MI (below).

WHEN LESS IS MORE

Traveling to an off-the-beaten-path park means fewer fellow visitors and more nature at its untouched finest. Here are the five least-visited national parks:

Gates of the Arctic, AK: Roughly 10,000

Kobuk Valley, AK: About 15,000

Lake Clark, AK: Around 17,000

Isle Royale, MI: Just over 26,600

North Cascades, WA: Approximately 30,000

Out of this World

Sometimes, nature is surreal. Other times, it's downright otherwordly. Here are a few national park landscapes that might make you feel like you've traveled to a galaxy far, far away.

① Death Valley National Park, CA/NV: America's hottest, lowest place fired the imagination of a young George Lucas, who thought it (along with locales in Tunisia) made the perfect stand-in for the harsh, lawless world of Tatooine in *Star Wars*. And so, C-3PO, R2-D2, and Jawas once roamed Death Valley's dunes and canyons.

② Everglades National Park, FL: Journalist Marjory Stoneman Douglas made a case for preserving these 1.5-million swampy acres by arguing that they were a vital "river of grass." Today, this extraordinary ecosystem is also a UNESCO World Heritage Site, an International Biosphere Reserve, and a Wetland of International Importance.

③ Yellowstone National Park, ID/MT/WY: When reports first came out about mud percolating like boiling water and rockets of steam and water exploding like clockwork, it was beyond the comprehension of most people. It's still hard to fathom that an underground reservoir of magma makes this one of Earth's most geologically dynamic places.

④ Bryce Canyon National Park, UT: Millions of years ago, siltstone, mudstone, and limestone accumulated beneath a lake. When the waters receded, the ancient rock remained, and, over millennia, was weathered into unusual pillar-like formations. From the first vista point to every other lookout beyond, Bryce Canyon's "forest" of hoodoos will mesmerize you.

NATIONAL
PARKS

Along the Anhinga Trail, Everglades National Park.

Badwater Basin salt flats in Death Valley National Park (left).

Chromatic Pool at the Upper Geyser Basin in Yellowstone National Park (below).

Thor's Hammer and hoodoos, Bryce Canyon National Park.

Tourism Contacts

On the road or before you go, log on to the official tourism website of your destination. These websites offer terrific ideas about organizing a visit and often include calendars of special events and activities. Prefer calling? Most states offer toll-free numbers.

UNITED STATES

Alabama Tourism Department
(800) 252-2262
(334) 242-4169
alabama.travel

Alaska Tourism
www.travelalaska.com

Arizona Office of Tourism
(866) 275-5816
(602) 364-3700
www.visitarizona.com

Arkansas Department of Parks, Heritage & Tourism
(800) 628-8725
(501) 682-7777
www.arkansas.com

California Travel & Toursm Commission
(916) 444-4429
www.visitcalifornia.com

Colorado Tourism Office
(800) 265-6723
www.colorado.com

Connecticut Office of Tourism
(888) 288-4748
(860) 500-2300
www.ctvisit.com

Delaware Tourism Office
(866) 284-7483
www.visitdelaware.com

Visit Florida
(888) 735-2872
(850) 488-5607
www.visitflorida.com

Explore Georgia
(800) 847-4842
www.exploregeorgia.org

Hawaii Tourism Authority
(800) 464-2924
(888) 297-9472 (from Canada)
www.gohawaii.com

Idaho Tourism
(800) 847-4843
(208) 334-2470
visitidaho.org

Illinois Bureau of Tourism
(312) 814-4732
www.enjoyillinois.com

Indiana Office of Tourism Development
(317) 232-8860
visitindiana.com

Iowa Tourism Office
(800) 345-4692
www.traveliowa.com

Kansas Tourism Office
(785) 296-2009
www.travelks.com

Kentucky Department of Tourism
(800) 225-8747
(502) 564-4930
www.kentuckytourism.com

Louisiana Office of Tourism
(800) 677-4082
(225) 635-0090
www.louisianatravel.com

Maine Office of Tourism
(888) 624-6345
(207) 624-7483
visitmaine.com

Maryland Office of Tourism Development
(877) 209-5883
www.visitmaryland.org

Massachusetts Office of Travel & Tourism
(800) 227-6277
(617) 973-8500
www.visitma.com

Pure Michigan
(888) 784-7328
www.michigan.org

Explore Minnesota
(888) 847-4866
(651) 556-8465
www.exploreminnesota.com

Visit Mississippi
(866) 733-6477
(601) 359-3129
visitmississippi.org

Missouri Division of Tourism
(573) 751-4133
www.visitmo.com

Montana Office of Tourism
(800) 847-4868
www.visitmt.com

Nebraska Tourism Commission
(402) 471-3796
visitnebraska.com

Travel Nevada
(775) 687-4322
travelnevada.com

New Hampshire Division of Travel and Tourism Development
(603) 271-2665
www.visitnh.gov

New Jersey Division of Travel and Tourism
(609) 599-6540
www.visitnj.org

New Mexico Tourism Department
(505) 827-7336
(505) 827-7400
www.newmexico.org

New York State Division of Tourism
(800) 225-5697
www.iloveny.com

Visit North Carolina
(800) 847-4862
www.visitnc.com

North Dakota Tourism Division
(800) 435-5663
(701) 328-2525
www.ndtourism.com

Tourism Ohio
(800) 282-5393
ohio.org

Oklahoma Tourism Department
(800) 652-6552
(405) 522-9500
www.travelok.com

Travel Oregon
(800) 547-7842
traveloregon.com

Pennsylvania Tourism Office
(800) 847-4872
visitpa.com

Visit Rhode Island
(800) 556-2484
www.visitrhodeisland.com

South Carolina Department of Parks, Recreation and Tourism
(803) 734-1700
discoversouthcarolina.com

South Dakota Department of Tourism
(605) 773-3301
www.travelsouthdakota.com

Tennessee Department of Tourist Development
(615) 741-2159
www.tnvacation.com

Texas Tourism
(512) 463-2000
(512) 936-0512
www.traveltexas.com

Visit Utah
(800) 200-1160
(801) 538-1900
www.visitutah.com

Vermont Department of Tourism & Marketing
(802) 828-3237
www.vermontvacation.com

Virginia Tourism Corporation
(800) 847-4882
www.virginia.org

Washington Tourism Alliance
(800) 544-1800
www.experiencewa.com

Destination DC
(202) 789-7000
washington.org

West Virginia Tourism Office
(800) 225-5982
(304) 558-2200
wvtourism.com

Wisconsin Department of Tourism
(800) 432-8747
(608) 266-2161
travelwisconsin.com

Wyoming Office of Tourism
(800) 225-5996
(307) 777-7777
travelwyoming.com

CANADA

Travel Alberta
(403) 648-1000
www.travelalberta.com

Destination British Columbia
(604) 660-2861
www.hellobc.com

Travel Manitoba
(800) 665-0040
(204) 927-7800
www.travelmanitoba.com

Tourism New Brunswick
(800) 561-0123
www.tourismnewbrunswick.ca

Newfoundland and Labrador Tourism
(800) 563-6353
(709) 729-2830
www.newfoundlandlabrador.com

Northwest Territories Tourism
(800) 661-0788
(867) 873-5007
spectacularnwt.com

Tourism Nova Scotia
(800) 565-0000
(902) 742-0511
www.novascotia.com

Ontario Tourism Marketing Partnership Corporation
(800) 668-2746
www.ontariotravel.net

Prince Edward Island Tourism
(800) 463-4734
(902) 437-8570
www.tourismpei.com

Tourisme Québec
(877) 266-5687
(514) 873-2015
www.bonjourquebec.com/en-ca

Tourism Saskatchewan
(877) 237-2273
(306) 787-9600
www.tourismsaskatchewan.com

Yukon Department of Tourism & Culture
(800) 661-0494
www.travelyukon.com

MEXICO

Mexico Tourism Board
www.visitmexico.com/en

PUERTO RICO

Discover Puerto Rico
(800) 866-7827
(787) 721-2400
www.discoverpuertorico.com
prtourism.com

UNITED STATES VIRGIN ISLANDS

Visit USVI
(800) 372-8784
www.visitusvi.com

Road Work

Road construction and road conditions resources

Get the Info from the 511 hotline

The U.S. Federal Highway Administration has begun implementing a national system of highway and road conditions/construction information for travelers. Under the plan, travelers can dial 511 and get up-to-date information on roads and highways.

Implementation of 511 is the responsibility of state and local agencies.

For more details, visit: www.fhwa.dot.gov/trafficinfo

UNITED STATES

Alabama
(888) 588-2848
algotraffic.com
www.dot.state.al.us

Alaska
511
(866) 282-7577
www.dot.state.ak.us

Arizona
511
(888) 411-7623
www.az511.com
www.azdot.gov

Arkansas
(501) 569-2374
www.idrivearkansas.com
www.arkansashighways.com

California
www.dot.ca.gov
roads.dot.ca.gov
(916) 654-2852
Eastern Sierras District 9:
511, (800) 427-7623
www.dot.ca.gov/d9
Inland Empire:
511, (877) 694-3511
www.ie511.org
Los Angeles/Orange/Ventura:
511, (877) 224-6511
go511.com
Sacramento/Northern Region:
511, (866) 511-8747
www.sacregion511.org
traffic.sacregion511.org
San Diego area:
511, (855) 467-3511
www.511sd.com
San Francisco Bay area:
511, (888) 500-4636
511.org
San Luis Obispo area:
511, (866) 928-8923

Colorado
511
(877) 315-7623 (in state)
(303) 639-1111 (out of state)
www.cotrip.org
www.codot.gov

Connecticut
(860) 594-2000
cttravelsmart.org
portal.ct.gov/DOT
www.i-84waterbury.com

Delaware
(800) 652-5600 (in state)
(302) 760-2080 (out of state)
www.deldot.gov

Florida
511
(866) 511-3352
fl511.com
fdot.gov

Georgia
511
(877) 694-2511
www.511ga.org

Hawaii
(808) 587-2220
hidot.hawaii.gov/highways/
  roadwork
O'ahu only:
511
www.goakamai.org

Idaho
511
(888) 432-7623
www.511.idaho.gov
www.itd.idaho.gov

Illinois
(800) 452-4368
www.gettingaroundillinois.com
idot.illinois.gov

Indiana
(800) 261-7623
pws.trafficwise.org/pws
indot.carsprogram.org
www.in.gov/indot/2420.htm

Iowa
511
(800) 288-1047
www.511ia.org
iowadot.gov

Kansas
511
(866) 511-5368
www.kandrive.org
www.ksdot.org

Kentucky
511
(866) 737-3767
goky.ky.gov
drive.ky.gov

Louisiana
511
(888) 762-3511
www.511la.org
www.dotd.la.gov

Maine
511
(207) 624-3000
newengland511.org
www.maine.gov/mdot

Maryland
511
(855) 466-3511
(410) 582-5605
chart.maryland.gov
www.roads.maryland.gov

Massachusetts
511
Metro Boston: (617) 986-5511
Central: (508) 499-5511
Western: 413) 754-5511
www.mass511.com

Michigan
(517) 241-2400
www.michigan.gov/drive
www.michigan.gov/mdot

Minnesota
511
(800) 542-0220
www.511mn.org
www.dot.state.mn.us

Mississippi
(866) 521-6368
www.mdottraffic.com

Missouri
(888) 275-6636
(573) 751-2551
traveler.modot.org/map
www.modot.org

Montana
511
(800) 226-7623
(406) 444-6200
roadreport.mdt.mt.gov
www.mdt.mt.gov/travinfo

Nebraska
511
(800) 906-9069
(402) 471-4567
www.511.nebraska.gov
dot.nebraska.gov

Nevada
511
(877) 687-6237
(775) 888-7000
nvroads.com/511-home
www.nevadadot.com

New Hampshire
(603) 271-6862
newengland511.org
www.nh.gov/dot

New Jersey
511
(866) 511-6538
www.511nj.org
www.state.nj.us/transportation

New Mexico
511
(800) 432-4269
(505) 795-1401
www.nmroads.com
www.dot.state.nm.us

New York
511
(888) 465-1169
www.511ny.org
www.dot.ny.gov
New York State Thruway:
(800) 847-8929
(518) 471-5300
www.thruway.ny.gov

North Carolina
511
(877) 511-4662
drivenc.gov
www.ncdot.gov/travel-maps

North Dakota
511
(866) 696-3511
www.dot.nd.gov/travel
travel.dot.nd.gov

Ohio
511
(855) 511-6446
www.ohgo.com
www.transportation.ohio.gov
Ohio Turnpike:
(888) 876-7453
www.ohioturnpike.org

Oklahoma
(844) 465-4997
okroads.org
www.ok.gov/odot

Oregon
511
(800) 977-6368
(503) 588-2941
(888) 275-6368
www.tripcheck.com
www.oregon.gov/odot

Pennsylvania
511
(877) 511-7366
www.511pa.com
www.penndot.gov

Rhode Island
(888) 401-4511
(844) 368-7623
(401) 222-2450
www.dot.ri.gov/travel

South Carolina
511
(877) 511-4672
(855) 467-2368
(803) 737-1200
www.511sc.org
www.scdot.org

South Dakota
511
(866) 697-3511
www.safetravelusa.com/sd
dot.sd.gov

Tennessee
511
(877) 244-0065
smartway.tn.gov
www.tn.gov/tdot/welcome-to-
  tennessee-511

Texas
(800) 452-9292
(877) 511-3255 (Dallas/Ft. Worth)
(512) 463-8588
www.drivetexas.org
511dfw.org
www.txdot.gov

Utah
511
(866) 511-8824
(801) 965-4000
udottraffic.utah.gov
www.udot.utah.gov

Vermont
newengland511.org
www.vtrans.vermont.gov

Virginia
511
(866) 695-1182
(800) 367-7623
www.511virginia.org
www.virginiadot.org/travel

Washington
511
(800) 695-7623
www.wsdot.com/traffic
www.wsdot.wa.gov/about/
  news/511/home

Washington, D.C.
311
(202) 673-6813
ddot.dc.gov

West Virginia
511
(855) 699-8511
www.wv511.org
transportation.wv.gov

Wisconsin
511
(866) 511-9472
511wi.gov

Wyoming
511
(888) 996-7623
www.wyoroad.info

CANADA

Alberta
511
(855) 391-9743
511.alberta.ca

British Columbia
(800) 550-4997
www.drivebc.ca
www2.gov.bc.ca/gov/content/
  transportation

Manitoba
511
(877) 627-6237 (in MB, SK, ON,
  and North Dakota)
(204) 945-3704
www.manitoba511.ca/en

New Brunswick
511
(800) 561-4063
www.gnb.ca/roads

Newfoundland & Labrador
511
(709) 729-2300
www.511nl.ca/en
www.gov.nl.ca/ti/roads/home

Northwest Territories
(800) 661-0750
www.dot.gov.nt.ca/Highways/
Highway-Conditions

Nova Scotia
511
In Canada, outside NS:
(888) 780-4440
511.novascotia.ca

Ontario
511
(866) 929-4257
511on.ca

Prince Edward Island
511
In Canada outside PEI:
(855) 241-2680
511.gov.pe.ca/en

Québec
511
(888) 355-0511
www.quebec511.info/en

Saskatchewan
(888) 335-7623 (in Canada)
Saskatoon area: (306) 933-8333
Regina area: (306) 787-7623
www.saskatchewan.ca/residents/
  transportation/highways/
  highway-hotline

Yukon Territory
511
(867) 667-5644
www.511yukon.ca

MEXICO

www.gob.mx

PUERTO RICO

(800) 981-3021
(787) 977-2200
its.dtop.gov.pr/en

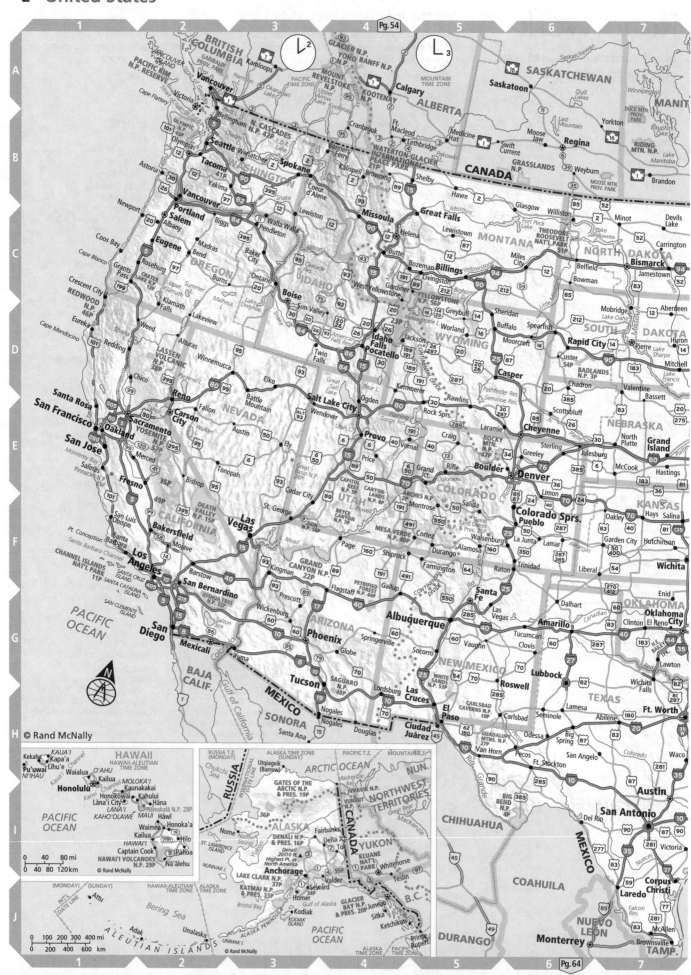

© Rand McNally

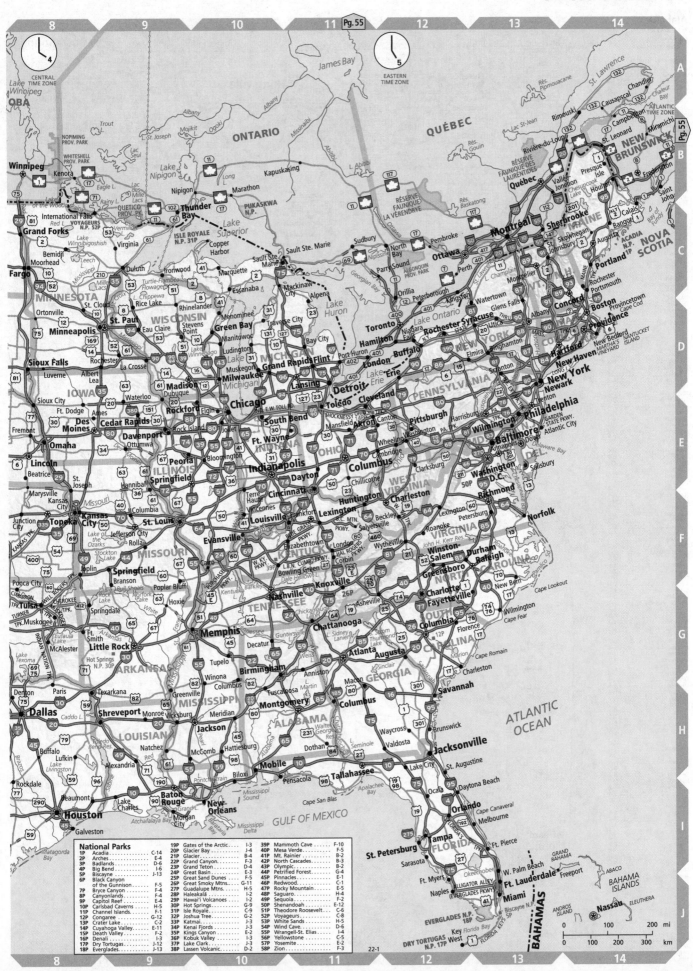

National Parks

1P	Acadia	C-14	
2P	Arches	E-4	
3P	Badlands	D-6	
4P	Big Bend	I-6	
5P	Biscayne	J-13	
6P	Black Canyon		
	of the Gunnison	F-5	
7P	Bryce Canyon	F-4	
8P	Canyonlands	E-4	
9P	Capitol Reef	E-4	
10P	Carlsbad Caverns	H-5	
11P	Channel Islands	F-1	
12P	Congaree	G-12	
13P	Crater Lake	C-2	
14P	Cuyahoga Valley	E-11	
15P	Death Valley	F-2	
16P	Denali	J-3	
17P	Dry Tortugas	J-12	
18P	Everglades	J-13	
19P	Gates of the Arctic	I-3	
20P	Glacier Bay	J-4	
21P	Glacier	B-4	
22P	Grand Canyon	F-3	
23P	Grand Teton	D-4	
24P	Great Basin	E-3	
25P	Great Sand Dunes	F-5	
26P	Great Smoky Mtns.	G-11	
27P	Guadalupe Mtns.	H-5	
28P	Haleakalā	I-2	
29P	Hawai'i Volcanoes	I-2	
30P	Hot Springs	G-9	
31P	Isle Royale	C-9	
32P	Joshua Tree	G-2	
33P	Katmai	J-3	
34P	Kenai Fjords	J-3	
35P	Kings Canyon	F-2	
36P	Kobuk Valley	I-3	
37P	Lake Clark	J-3	
38P	Lassen Volcanic	D-2	
39P	Mammoth Cave	F-10	
40P	Mesa Verde	F-5	
41P	Mt. Rainier	B-2	
42P	North Cascades	B-3	
43P	Olympic	B-2	
44P	Petrified Forest	G-4	
45P	Pinnacles	E-1	
46P	Redwood	C-1	
47P	Rocky Mountain	E-5	
48P	Saguaro	H-4	
49P	Sequoia	F-2	
50P	Shenandoah	E-12	
51P	Theodore Roosevelt	C-6	
52P	Voyageurs	C-8	
53P	White Sands	H-5	
54P	Wind Cave	D-6	
55P	Wrangell-St. Elias	I-4	
56P	Yellowstone	C-5	
57P	Yosemite	E-2	
58P	Zion	F-3	

4 Alabama

Alabama
Population: 4,779,736
Land Area: 50,645 sq. mi.
Capital: Montgomery

Cities and Towns

Abbeville	H-6
Alabaster	D-3
Albertville	B-4
Alexander City	E-5
Aliceville	E-1
Andalusia	H-4
Anniston	C-5
Arab	B-4
Ashland	D-5
Ashville	C-4
Athens	A-3
Atmore	I-2
Attalla	C-4
Auburn	F-5
Bay Minette	I-2
Bessemer	D-3
Birmingham	D-3
Boaz	B-4
Brent	E-3
Brewton	H-3
Bridgeport	A-5
Butler	G-1
Calera	E-3
Camden	G-3
Carrollton	D-1
Centre	C-5
Centreville	E-3
Chatom	H-1
Childersburg	D-4
Citronelle	H-1
Clanton	E-3
Clayton	G-6
Columbiana	D-4
Cullman	B-3
Dadeville	E-5
Daleville	H-5
Daphne	I-1
Decatur	B-3
Demopolis	F-2
Dothan	H-6
Double Springs	C-2
East Brewton	H-3
Elba	H-5
Enterprise	H-5
Eufaula	G-6
Eutaw	E-2
Evergreen	H-3
Fairhope	J-1
Fayette	C-2
Florence	A-2
Foley	J-2
Fort Payne	B-5
Fultondale	D-3
Gadsden	C-5
Geneva	I-5
Greensboro	E-2
Greenville	G-4
Grove Hill	G-2
Guin	C-2
Gulf Shores	J-2
Guntersville	B-4
Haleyville	C-1
Hamilton	C-1
Hanceville	B-3
Hartford	H-5
Hartselle	B-3
Hayneville	F-4
Hazel Green	A-4
Headland	H-6
Heflin	C-5
Henagar	B-5
Homewood	D-3
Hoover	D-3
Huntsville	A-4
Irondale	D-3
Jackson	H-2
Jacksonville	C-5
Jasper	C-3
LaFayette	E-6
Lanett	E-6
Leeds	D-4
Lincoln	D-4
Linden	F-2
Lineville	D-5
Livingston	F-1
Luverne	G-4
Madison	A-3
Marion	E-2
Midfield	D-3
Mobile	I-1
Monroeville	H-2
Montevallo	E-3
Montgomery	F-4
Moulton	B-3
Muscle Shoals	A-2
Northport	D-2
Oneonta	C-4
Opelika	E-6
Opp	H-4
Orange Beach	J-2
Oxford	D-5
Ozark	H-5
Pelham	D-3
Pell City	D-4
Phenix City	F-6
Piedmont	C-5
Pinson	C-4
Prattville	F-4
Prichard	I-1
Rainbow City	C-5
Rainsville	B-5
Red Bay	B-1
Roanoke	D-6
Robertsdale	J-2
Rockford	E-4
Russellville	B-2
Saraland	I-1
Scottsboro	B-5
Selma	F-3
Sheffield	A-2
Spanish Fort	I-1
Springville	C-4
Sumiton	C-3
Sylacauga	D-4
Talladega	D-4
Tallassee	F-5
Theodore	I-1
Thomasville	G-2
Troy	G-5
Trussville	D-3
Tuscaloosa	D-2
Tuscumbia	A-2
Tuskegee	F-5
Union Springs	F-5
Valley	E-6
Vernon	C-1
Warrior	C-3
Wedowee	D-5
Wetumpka	F-4
Winfield	C-2
York	F-1

NOTE: Maps are not always in alphabetical order.
See Page 1 for map location in this atlas.

Alaska • Hawaii   5

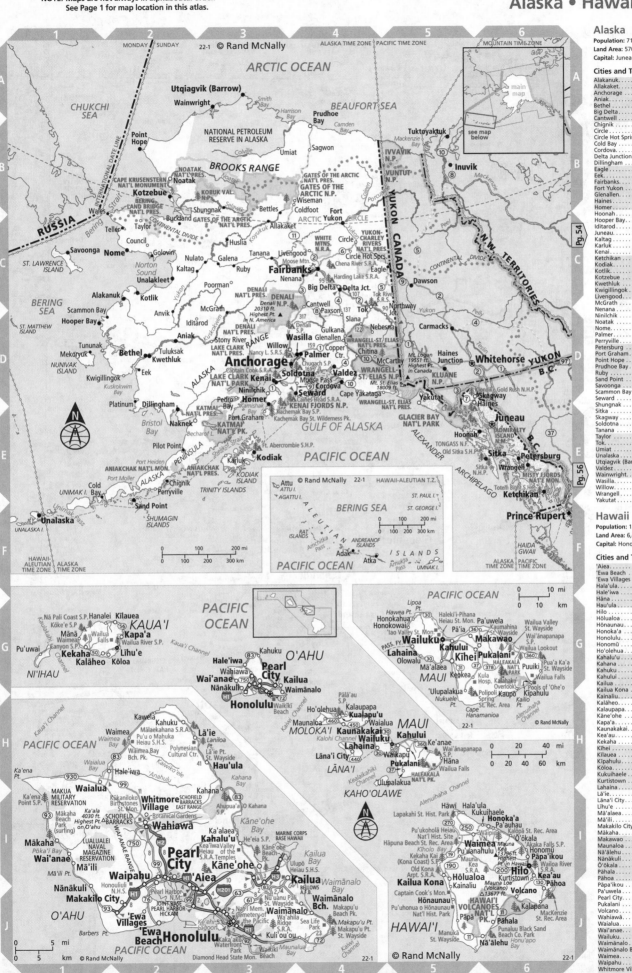

Alaska
Population: 710,231
Land Area: 570,641 sq. mi.
Capital: Juneau

Cities and Towns

Alakanuk C-2
Allakaket C-3
Anchorage D-3
Aniak D-2
Bethel D-2
Big Delta C-4
Cantwell C-4
Chignik E-2
Circle C-4
Circle Hot Springs C-4
Cold Bay E-1
Cordova D-4
Delta Junction C-4
Dillingham E-2
Eagle C-5
Eek D-2
Fairbanks C-4
Fort Yukon C-4
Glenallen D-4
Haines D-5
Homer D-3
Hoonah E-6
Hooper Bay D-1
Iditarod D-2
Juneau E-6
Kaltag C-2
Karluk E-3
Kenai D-3
Ketchikan E-6
Kodiak E-3
Kotlik C-2
Kotzebue B-2
Kwethluk D-2
Kwigillingok D-2
Livengood C-4
McGrath D-3
Nenana C-4
Ninilchik D-3
Noatak B-2
Nome C-2
Palmer D-4
Perryville E-2
Petersburg E-6
Port Graham E-3
Point Hope B-2
Prudhoe Bay B-4
Ruby C-3
Sand Point F-2
Savoonga C-1
Scammon Bay D-1
Seward D-4
Shungnak B-3
Sitka E-5
Skagway D-5
Soldotna D-3
Tanana C-3
Taylor C-2
Tok D-4
Umiat B-3
Unalaska F-1
Utqiagvik (Barrow) A-3
Valdez D-4
Wainwright A-3
Wasilla D-4
Willow D-3
Wrangell E-6
Yakutat D-5

Hawaii
Population: 1,360,301
Land Area: 6,423 sq. mi.
Capital: Honolulu

Cities and Towns

'Aiea J-2
'Ewa Beach J-2
'Ewa Villages J-2
Hala'ula I-5
Hale'iwa H-2
Hāna H-5
Hau'ula H-3
Hilo I-6
Hōlualoa J-5
Hōnaunau J-5
Honoka'a I-6
Honolulu J-3
Honomū I-6
Ho'olehua H-4
Kahalu'u I-3
Kahana I-3
Kahuku H-2
Kahului G-5
Kailua I-3
Kailua Kona I-5
Kainaliu J-5
Kalāheo G-1
Kalaupapa H-4
Kāne'ohe I-3
Kapa'a G-2
Kaunakakai H-4
Kea'au I-6
Kekaha G-1
Kīhei G-5
Kīlauea G-2
Kīpahulu G-6
Kōloa G-1
Kukuihaele I-6
Kurtistown I-6
Lahaina G-5
Lā'ie H-2
Lāna'i City H-4
Līhu'e G-2
Mā'alaea G-5
Mā'ili I-1
Makakilo City J-2
Mākaha I-1
Makawao G-6
Maunaloa H-4
Nā'ālehu J-6
Nānākuli J-1
O'ōkala I-6
Pāhala J-6
Pāhoa J-6
Pāpa'ikou I-6
Pa'uwela G-6
Pearl City I-2
Pukalani G-5
Volcano J-6
Wahiawā I-2
Waialua H-1
Wai'anae I-1
Wailuku G-5
Waimānalo J-4
Waimānalo Beach J-4
Waimea H-2
Waipahu I-2
Whitmore Village I-2

© Rand McNally

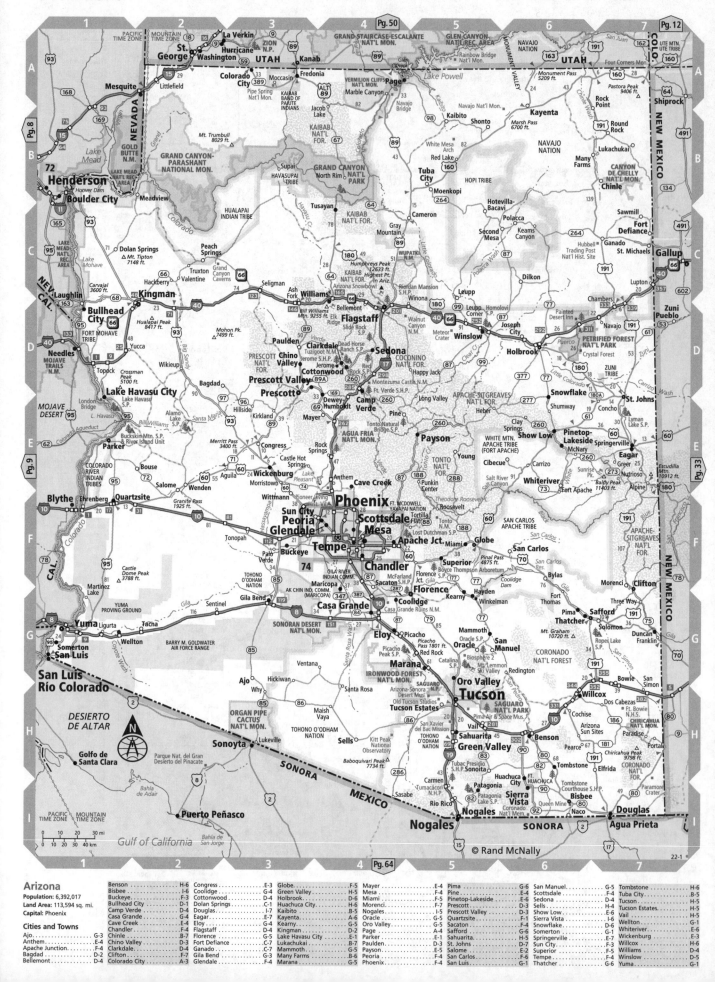

Arizona
Population: 6,392,017
Land Area: 113,594 sq. mi.
Capital: Phoenix

Cities and Towns

Ajo	G-3
Anthem	E-4
Apache Junction	F-4
Bagdad	D-2
Bellemont	D-4

Benson	H-6
Bisbee	I-6
Buckeye	F-3
Bullhead City	D-1
Camp Verde	D-4
Casa Grande	G-4
Cave Creek	E-4
Chandler	F-4
Chino Valley	D-3
Clarkdale	D-4
Clifton	F-7
Colorado City	A-3

Congress	E-3
Coolidge	G-4
Cottonwood	D-4
Dolan Springs	C-1
Douglas	I-7
Eagar	E-7
Eloy	G-4
Flagstaff	D-4
Florence	G-5
Fort Defiance	C-7
Ganado	C-7
Gila Bend	G-3
Glendale	F-4

Globe	F-5
Green Valley	H-5
Holbrook	D-6
Huachuca City	H-6
Kaibito	B-5
Kayenta	A-6
Kearny	G-5
Kingman	D-2
Lake Havasu City	E-1
Lukachukai	B-7
Mammoth	G-5
Many Farms	B-6
Marana	G-5

Mayer	E-4
Mesa	F-4
Miami	F-5
Morenci	F-7
Nogales	I-5
Oracle	G-5
Oro Valley	G-5
Page	A-4
Parker	E-1
Payson	E-5
Peoria	F-4
Phoenix	F-4

Pima	G-6
Pine	E-4
Pinetop-Lakeside	E-6
Prescott	D-3
Prescott Valley	D-3
Quartzsite	F-1
Safford	G-6
Sahuarita	H-5
St. Johns	D-7
Salome	E-2
San Carlos	F-5
San Luis	G-1

San Manuel	G-5
Scottsdale	F-4
Sedona	D-4
Sells	H-4
Show Low	E-6
Sierra Vista	I-6
Snowflake	D-6
Somerton	G-1
Springerville	E-7
Sun City	F-3
Superior	F-5
Tempe	F-4
Thatcher	G-6

Tombstone	H-6
Tuba City	B-5
Tucson	H-5
Tucson Estates	H-5
Vail	H-6
Wellton	G-1
Whiteriver	E-6
Wickenburg	E-3
Willcox	H-6
Williams	D-4
Winslow	D-5
Yuma	G-1

© Rand McNally

NOTE: Maps are not always in alphabetical order.
See Page 1 for map location in this atlas.

Arkansas 7

Pg. 20
Pg. 27
Pg. 28
Pg. 23
Pg. 42
Pg. 47

© Rand McNally

Arkansas

Population: 2,915,918
Land Area: 52,035 sq. mi.
Capital: Little Rock

Cities and Towns

Arkadelphia E-3
Ashdown A-6
Ash Flat F-6
Ashdown B-6
Batesville C-6
Bella Vista A-1
Benton D-4
Bentonville A-2
Berryville B-8
Booneville C-2
Cabot D-6
Camden F-4
Charleston C-2
Clarendon D-7
Clarksville C-3
Clinton C-4
Conway C-4
Corning A-7
Crossett G-5
Danville C-3
Dardanelle C-3
De Valls Bluff D-6
De Queen E-1
De Witt D-6
Dumas E-6
El Dorado F-4
Eureka Springs A-2
Fayetteville A-2
Fordyce E-4
Forrest City C-7
Fort Smith C-1
Hamburg G-5
Hampton F-4
Harrison A-3
Harrisburg C-7
Heber Springs C-5
Helena-W. Helena D-7
Hope E-2
Hot Springs D-3
Hot Springs Village D-3
Huntsville B-2
Jacksonville D-5
Jasper B-3
Jonesboro B-7
Lake Village F-6
Lewisville F-2
Little Rock D-4
Lonoke D-5
Magnolia F-3
Malvern D-4
Marianna D-7
Marshall B-4
McGehee F-6
Melbourne B-5
Mena D-1
Monticello F-5
Morrilton C-4
Mount Ida D-2
Mountain Home A-4
Mountain View B-5
Murfreesboro E-2
Nashville E-2
Newport C-6
North Little Rock D-4
Osceola B-8
Paragould A-7
Paris C-2
Perryville C-4
Piggott A-8
Pine Bluff E-5
Pocahontas A-7
Prescott E-3
Rison F-5
Rogers A-2
Russellville C-3
Salem A-5
Searcy C-5
Sheridan E-4
Siloam Springs A-1
Springdale A-2
Star City F-5
Stuttgart D-6
Texarkana F-2
Trumann B-7
Van Buren C-1
Waldron D-2
Walnut Ridge B-7
Warren F-5
West Memphis C-8
Wynne C-7
Yellville A-4

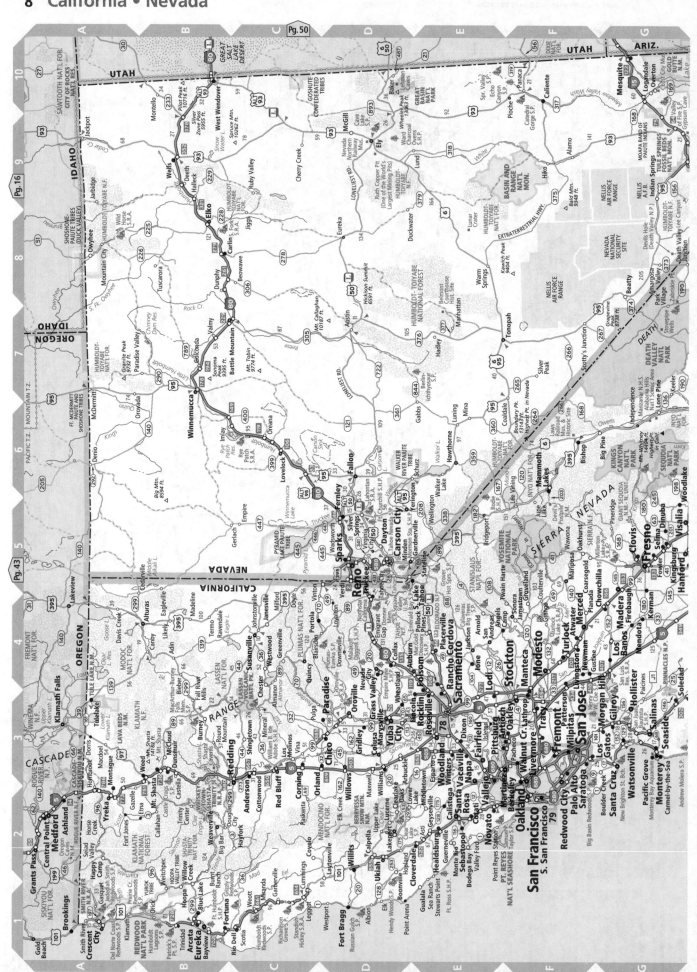

NOTE: Maps are not always in alphabetical order.
See Page 1 for map location in this atlas.

California • Nevada   9

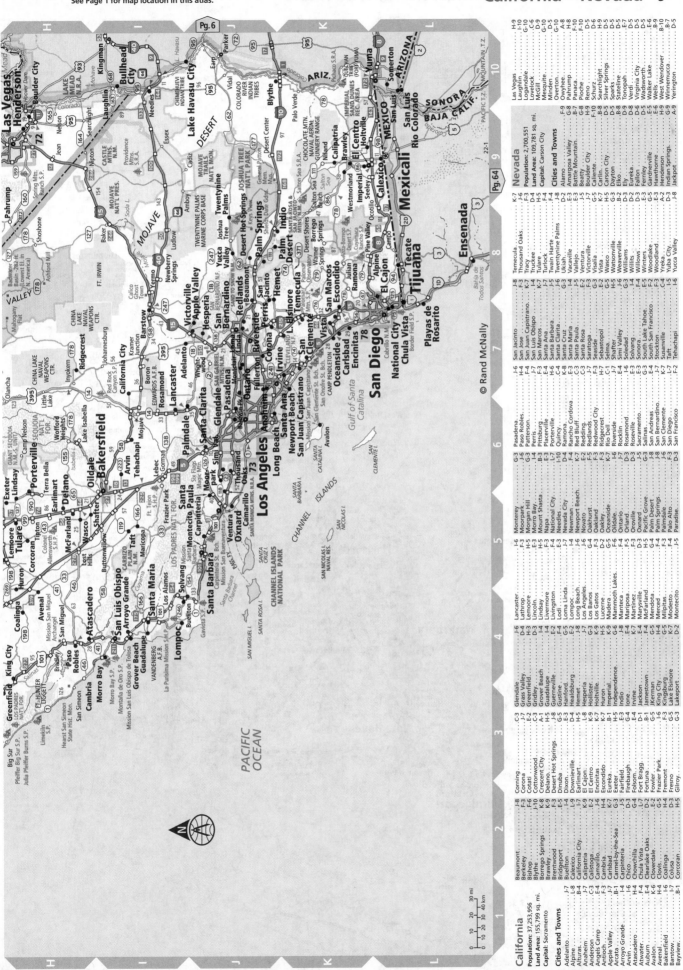

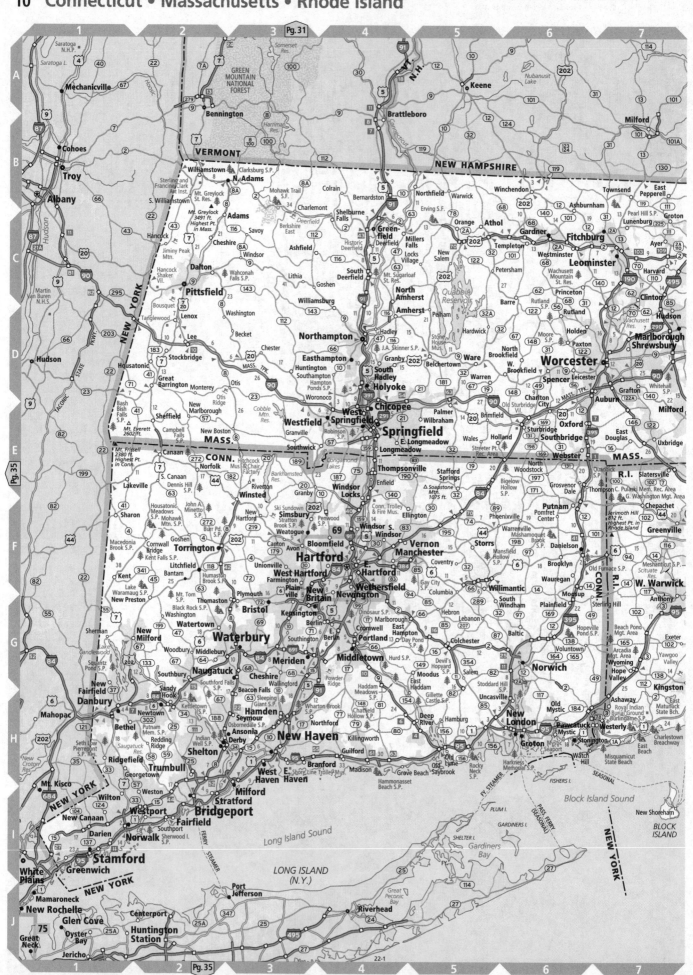

NOTE: Maps are not always in alphabetical order.
See Page 1 for map location in this atlas.

Connecticut • Massachusetts • Rhode Island 11

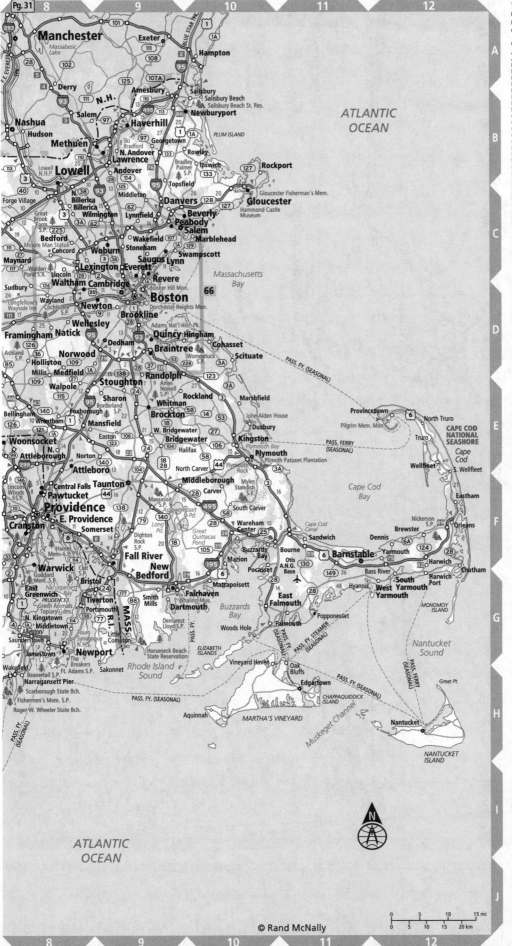

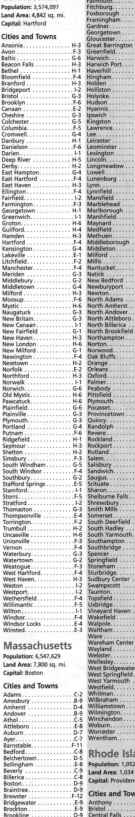

Connecticut
Population: 3,574,097
Land Area: 4,842 sq. mi.
Capital: Hartford

Cities and Towns
Ansonia....H-3
Avon....H-3
Baltic....G-6
Beacon Falls....H-3
Bethel....H-1
Bloomfield....F-4
Branford....H-3
Bridgeport....I-2
Bristol....G-3
Brooklyn....F-6
Canaan....E-2
Cheshire....G-3
Colchester....G-5
Columbia....F-5
Cromwell....G-4
Danbury....H-1
Danielson....F-6
Darien....I-1
Deep River....H-5
Derby....H-2
East Hampton....G-4
East Hartford....F-4
East Haven....H-3
Ellington....F-5
Fairfield....I-2
Farmington....F-3
Georgetown....H-1
Greenwich....I-1
Groton....H-6
Guilford....H-4
Hamden....H-3
Hartford....F-4
Kensington....G-4
Lakeville....E-1
Litchfield....F-2
Manchester....F-4
Meriden....G-3
Middlebury....G-2
Middletown....G-4
Milford....H-3
Moosup....F-6
Mystic....H-6
Naugatuck....G-3
New Britain....G-3
New Canaan....I-1
New Fairfield....G-1
New Haven....H-3
New London....H-6
New Milford....G-1
Newington....F-4
Newtown....H-2
Norfolk....E-2
Northford....H-3
Norwalk....I-1
Norwich....H-6
Old Mystic....H-6
Pawcatuck....H-6
Plainfield....F-6
Plainville....G-3
Plymouth....G-3
Portland....G-4
Putnam....F-6
Ridgefield....H-1
Seymour....H-3
Shelton....H-2
Simsbury....F-3
South Windham....G-5
South Windsor....F-4
Southbury....G-2
Stafford Springs....E-5
Stamford....I-1
Storrs....F-5
Stratford....I-2
Thomaston....G-3
Thompsonville....E-4
Torrington....F-2
Trumbull....H-2
Uncasville....H-6
Unionville....F-3
Vernon....F-4
Waterbury....G-2
Watertown....G-2
Weatogue....F-3
West Hartford....F-4
West Haven....H-3
Weston....I-2
Westport....I-2
Wethersfield....F-4
Willimantic....F-5
Wilton....I-1
Windsor....E-4
Windsor Locks....E-4
Winsted....E-3

Massachusetts
Population: 6,547,629
Land Area: 7,800 sq. mi.
Capital: Boston

Cities and Towns
Adams....C-2
Amesbury....B-9
Amherst....D-4
Andover....B-9
Athol....C-5
Attleboro....E-8
Auburn....D-7
Ayer....C-7
Barnstable....F-11
Bedford....C-8
Belchertown....D-5
Bellingham....E-8
Beverly....C-9
Billerica....C-8
Boston....D-9
Braintree....D-9
Brewster....F-12
Bridgewater....E-9
Brockton....E-9
Brookline....D-9
Buzzards Bay....F-10
Cambridge....D-9
Chicopee....E-4
Clinton....C-7
Cohasset....D-10
Concord....C-8
Dalton....C-2
Danvers....C-9
Dartmouth....G-9
Dedham....D-9
Dennis....F-12
East Douglas....E-7
East Falmouth....G-11
East Longmeadow....E-4
East Pepperell....B-7
Easthampton....D-4
Edgartown....H-11
Everett....C-9
Fairhaven....G-9
Fall River....F-9
Falmouth....G-10
Fitchburg....C-7
Foxborough....E-8
Framingham....D-8
Gardner....C-6
Georgetown....B-9
Gloucester....C-10
Great Barrington....D-2
Greenfield....C-4
Harwich....F-12
Harwich Port....G-12
Haverhill....B-9
Hingham....D-9
Holden....D-6
Holliston....D-8
Holyoke....D-4
Hudson....D-7
Hyannis....G-11
Ipswich....B-10
Kingston....E-10
Lawrence....B-9
Lee....D-2
Leicester....D-6
Leominster....C-7
Lexington....C-8
Lincoln....C-8
Longmeadow....E-4
Lowell....B-8
Lunenburg....C-7
Lynn....C-9
Lynnfield....C-9
Mansfield....E-8
Marblehead....C-10
Marlborough....D-7
Marshfield....E-10
Maynard....C-8
Medfield....D-8
Medford....C-9
Methuen....B-9
Middleborough....F-9
Middleton....C-9
Milford....E-8
Millis....D-8
Nantucket....H-12
Natick....D-8
New Bedford....G-9
Newburyport....B-10
Newton....D-9
North Adams....B-3
North Amherst....C-4
North Andover....B-9
North Attleboro....E-8
North Billerica....C-8
North Brookfield....D-6
Northampton....D-4
Norton....E-9
Norwood....D-9
Oak Bluffs....G-11
Orange....C-5
Orleans....F-12
Oxford....E-6
Palmer....E-5
Peabody....C-9
Pittsfield....C-2
Plymouth....E-10
Pocasset....F-10
Provincetown....E-12
Quincy....D-9
Randolph....D-9
Revere....C-9
Rockland....E-9
Rockport....B-10
Rutland....D-6
Salem....C-9
Salisbury....B-10
Sandwich....F-11
Saugus....C-9
Scituate....D-10
Sharon....E-9
Shelburne Falls....C-4
Shrewsbury....D-7
Smith Mills....G-9
Somerset....F-9
South Deerfield....C-4
South Hadley....D-4
South Yarmouth....G-12
Southampton....D-4
Southbridge....E-6
Spencer....D-6
Springfield....E-4
Stoneham....C-9
Sturbridge....E-6
Sudbury Center....D-8
Swampscott....C-9
Taunton....F-9
Topsfield....B-9
Uxbridge....E-7
Vineyard Haven....G-10
Wakefield....C-9
Walpole....D-8
Waltham....D-8
Ware....D-5
Wareham Center....F-10
Wayland....D-8
Webster....E-6
Wellesley....D-8
West Bridgewater....E-9
West Springfield....E-4
West Yarmouth....G-12
Westfield....E-4
Whitman....E-9
Wilbraham....E-5
Williamstown....B-2
Wilmington....C-9
Winchendon....B-6
Woburn....C-9
Worcester....D-7
Wrentham....E-8

Rhode Island
Population: 1,052,567
Land Area: 1,034 sq. mi.
Capital: Providence

Cities and Towns
Anthony....F-7
Bristol....G-8
Central Falls....F-8
Cranston....F-8
East Greenwich....F-8
East Providence....F-8
Exeter....G-7
Greenville....F-7
Jamestown....G-8
Kingston....G-8
Middletown....G-8
Narragansett Pier....H-8
Newport....G-8
North Kingstown....G-8
Pawtucket....F-8
Portsmouth....G-8
Providence....F-8
Tiverton....G-9
Warwick....F-8
West Warwick....F-8
Westerly....H-7
Woonsocket....E-8

© Rand McNally

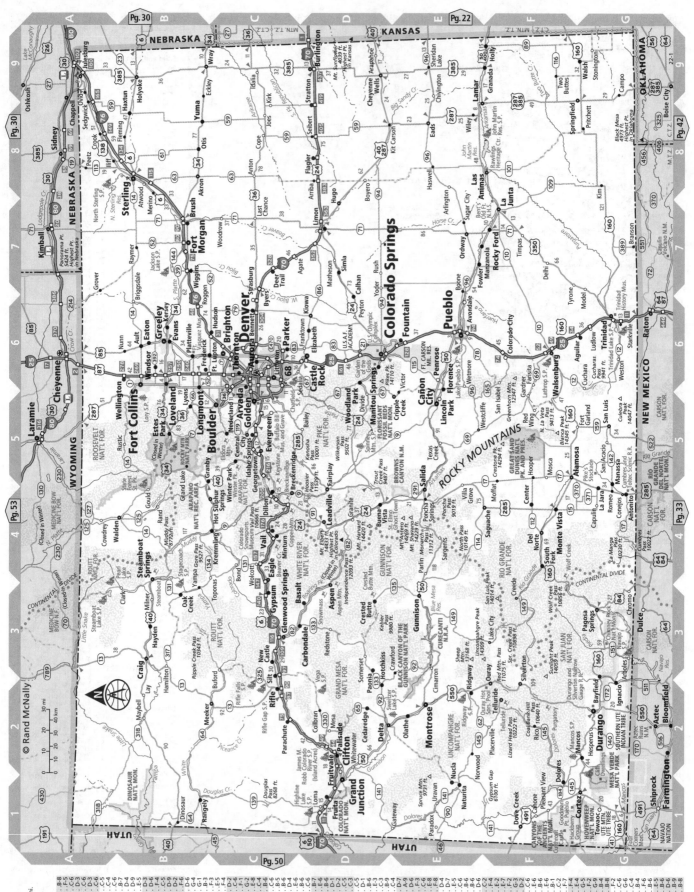

Colorado

Population: 5,029,196
Land Area: 103,642 sq. mi.
Capital: Denver

Cities and Towns

Akron B-8
Alamosa F-5
Arvada C-6
Aspen D-4
Aurora C-6
Basalt D-3
Bennett C-6
Boulder C-5
Breckenridge ... C-5
Brighton C-6
Brush B-7
Buena Vista D-4
Burlington C-9
Cañon City E-5
Carbondale D-3
Castle Rock C-6
Center F-4
Central City ... C-5
Cheyenne Wells . C-9
Colorado City .. E-6
Colorado Springs D-6
Conejos G-4
Cortez G-1
Craig B-3
Creede F-4
Cripple Creek .. D-5
Del Norte F-4
Delta E-2
Denver C-6
Dove Creek F-1
Durango G-2
Eads D-8
Eagle D-4
Englewood C-6
Estes Park B-5
Evans B-6
Fairplay D-5
Florence E-5
Fort Collins ... B-5
Fort Morgan B-7
Fountain D-6
Frederick B-6
Fruita D-1
Fruitvale D-1
Glenwood Springs D-3
Golden C-6
Granby C-4
Grand Junction . D-1
Greeley B-6
Gunnison E-3
Gypsum D-3
Holyoke A-9
Hot Sulphur Springs C-4
Julesburg A-9
Kiowa C-6
La Junta E-7
Lake City E-3
Lakewood C-6
Lamar D-8
Las Animas E-7
Leadville D-4
Limon C-7
Lincoln Park ... E-5
Littleton C-6
Longmont B-6
Loveland B-5
Manitou Springs D-6
Mancos G-2
Meeker C-2
Monte Vista F-4
Montrose E-2
Ordway D-7
Ouray E-2
Pagosa Springs . G-3
Palisade D-1
Parker C-6
Penrose E-5
Platteville B-6
Pueblo E-6
Rangely C-1
Rifle D-2
Rocky Ford E-7
Saguache E-4
Salida E-4
Silverton F-2
Springfield E-9
Steamboat Springs B-4
Sterling B-8
Telluride F-2
Thornton C-6
Towaoc G-1
Trinidad F-6
Vail D-4
Walden B-4
Walsenburg F-6
Wellington B-5
Westcliffe E-5
Windsor B-6
Woodland Park .. D-6
Wray B-9
Yuma B-8

NOTE: Maps are not always in alphabetical order.
See Page 1 for map location in this atlas.

Delaware • Maryland 13

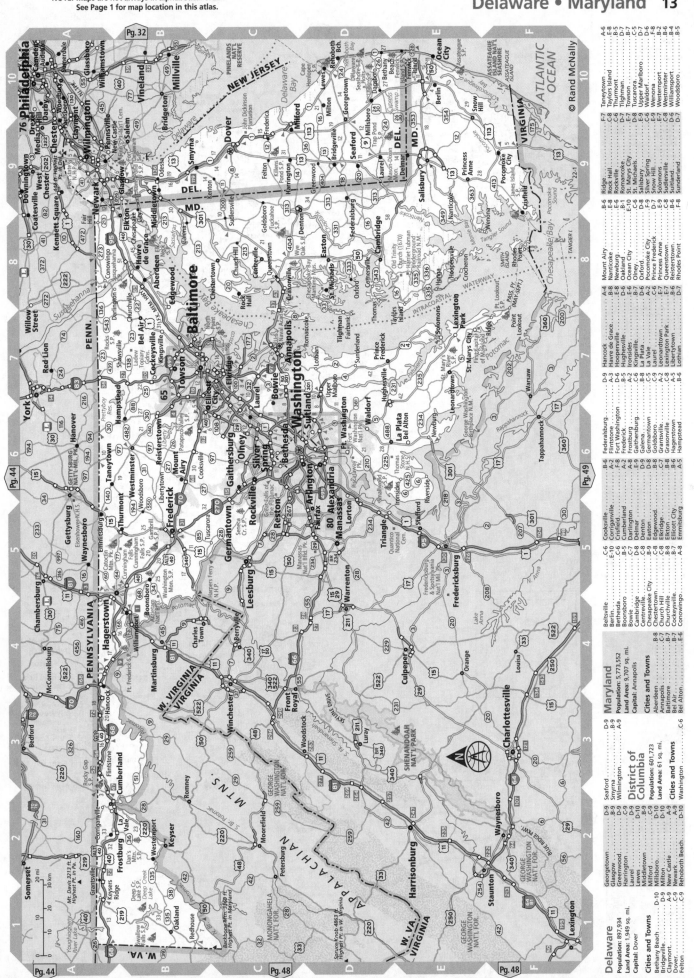

© Rand McNally

Taneytown F-7
Taylors Island C-8
Thurmont C-6
Tilghman D-7
Towson E-7
Tuscarora C-5
Upper Marlboro B-6
Wenona E-9
Westernport E-7
Westminster D-6
Williamsport B-5
Woodsboro D-7

Ridge B-6
Rock Hall E-8
Rockville E-6
Romancoke B-1
St. Marys City C-6
St. Michaels D-8
Salisbury D-9
Silver Spring E-6
Snow Hill F-8
Solomons B-2
Sudlersville B-6
Sunderland B-5

Mount Airy A-4
Nanticoke E-8
Newburg F-8
Oakland D-6
Ocean City E-10
Olney D-6
Oxford D-8
Pocomoke City A-2
Poolesville C-6
Princess Anne E-7
Queenstown D-8
Reisterstown D-6
Rhodes Point D-7

Hancock D-9
Havre de Grace A-3
Hoopersville B-5
Hughesville F-8
Ironsides E-9
Kingsville B-8
La Plata C-5
La Vale C-6
Laurel C-6
Leonardtown E-9
Lexington Park E-7
Libertytown C-8
Lothian B-6

Federalsburg B-6
Flintstone A-2
Fort Washington F-8
Frederick A-2
Frostburg E-9
Galena E-8
Germantown D-8
Goldsboro C-8
Grasonville B-6
Hagerstown A-5
Hampstead A-8

Cooksville C-6
Cordova E-10
Crisfield B-5
Cumberland C-7
Darlington D-8
Delmar D-8
Denton B-9
Easton C-5
Eldridge C-8
Elkridge B-8
Ellicott City B-7
Emmitsburg A-8

Beltsville B-8
Berlin E-10
Bethesda B-9
Boonsboro C-7
Bowie D-8
Cambridge B-9
Centreville C-5
Chesapeake City .. B-8
Chestertown C-8
Church Hill C-7
Clinton B-7
Cockeysville E-6
Conowingo C-9

Maryland
Population: 5,773,552
Land Area: 9,707 sq. mi.
Capital: Annapolis

Cities and Towns
Aberdeen C-9
Annapolis D-10
Baltimore A-9
Bel Alton C-6

Delaware
Population: 897,934
Land Area: 1,949 sq. mi.
Capital: Dover

Cities and Towns
Bethany Beach D-10
Bridgeville D-9
Claymont A-9
Dover C-9
Felton C-9

Georgetown D-9
Glasgow B-9
Greenwood C-9
Laurel D-10
Lewes C-9
Middletown B-9
Milford C-9
Millsboro D-10
Milton D-9
New Castle A-9
Newark A-9
Rehoboth Beach .. C-9

Seaford D-9
Smyrna B-9
Wilmington A-9

District of Columbia
Population: 601,723
Land Area: 61 sq. mi.

Cities and Towns
Washington D-10

Florida
Population: 18,801,310
Land Area: 53,625 sq. mi.
Capital: Tallahassee

Cities and Towns
Altamonte Springs...... D-4
Apalachicola............ I-3
Arcadia................. F-4
Atlantic Beach.......... B-4
Bartow................. E-4
Belle Glade............ G-5
Blountstown............ H-3
Boca Raton............. G-6
Bonifay................ H-3
Bradenton............. F-3
Brandon............... E-3
Brooksville............ D-3
Bunnell............... C-4
Bushnell.............. D-4
Cape Canaveral........ E-5
Cape Coral............ G-4
Chipley............... H-3
Clearwater............ E-3
Clermont.............. D-4
Cocoa Beach.......... E-5
Coral Gables.......... H-6
Crawfordville......... B-1
Crestview............. H-2
Cross City............ C-2
Dade City............. D-3
Dania Beach.......... H-6
Daytona Beach........ D-5
De Funiak Springs..... H-2
DeBary............... D-4
Deerfield Beach....... G-6
DeLand............... D-4
Delray Beach......... G-6
Dunedin.............. E-3
Edgewater............ D-5
Englewood............ F-3
Eustis................ D-4
Fernandina Beach...... B-4
Fort Lauderdale....... H-6
Fort Myers............ G-4
Fort Pierce........... F-6
Fort Walton Beach..... H-2
Gainesville........... C-3
Green Cove Springs.... C-4
Haines City........... E-4
Hallandale Beach...... H-6
Hialeah............... H-6
Holly Hill............. C-5
Hollywood............ H-6
Homestead............ H-6
Homosassa............ D-3
Homosassa Springs.... D-3
Hudson............... E-3
Immokalee............ G-4
Inverness............. D-3
Jacksonville.......... B-4
Jacksonville Beach.... B-4
Jasper............... B-3
Jensen Beach......... F-6
Jupiter............... F-6
Kendall............... H-6
Key Largo............ I-6
Key West............. J-4
Kissimmee............ E-4
La Belle.............. G-4
Lady Lake............ D-4
Lake Buena Vista...... E-4
Lake Butler........... B-3
Lake City............. B-3
Lake Wales........... E-4
Lake Worth........... G-6
Lakeland............. E-4
Largo................ E-3
Leesburg............. D-4
Lehigh Acres......... G-4
Live Oak............. B-3
Lutz................. E-3
Macclenny............ B-3
Madeira Beach........ E-3
Madison.............. B-2
Marathon............. I-5
Marco................ H-4
Marianna............. H-3
Melbourne............ E-5
Miami................ H-6
Miami Beach.......... H-6
Middleburg........... B-4
Milton............... H-1
Monticello........... B-2
Moore Haven......... G-5
Naples............... H-4
New Port Richey...... E-3
New Smyrna Beach.... D-5
North Palm Beach..... G-6
Ocala............... D-3
Okeechobee.......... F-5
Orange Park.......... B-4
Orlando.............. D-4
Ormond Beach........ C-5
Palatka.............. C-4
Palm Bay............. E-5
Palm Beach.......... G-6
Palm Coast.......... C-4
Palmetto............ F-3
Panama City.......... I-3
Pensacola........... H-1
Perry............... B-2
Plant City........... E-3
Pompano Beach...... G-6
Port Charlotte....... F-4
Port Orange......... D-5
Port St. Joe......... I-3
Port St. Lucie....... F-6
Punta Gorda......... G-4
Quincy.............. B-1
St. Augustine........ C-4
St. Cloud............ E-4
St. Pete Beach....... E-3
St. Petersburg....... E-3
Sanford............. D-4
Sarasota............ F-3
Sebastian........... E-5
Sebring............. F-5
Starke.............. C-4
Stuart.............. F-6
Sunrise............. H-6
Tallahassee......... B-1
Tampa.............. E-3
Tarpon Springs...... E-3
Tavares............. D-4
Titusville........... D-5
Trenton............. C-3
Venice.............. F-3
Vero Beach......... F-6
Warrington......... H-1
Wauchula........... F-4
West Palm Beach.... G-6
Weston............. H-6
Winter Garden...... D-4
Winter Haven....... E-4
Yeehaw Junction.... E-5
Zephyrhills......... E-3

© Rand McNally

© Rand McNally

NOTE: Maps are not always in alphabetical order.
See Page 1 for map location in this atlas.

Georgia 15

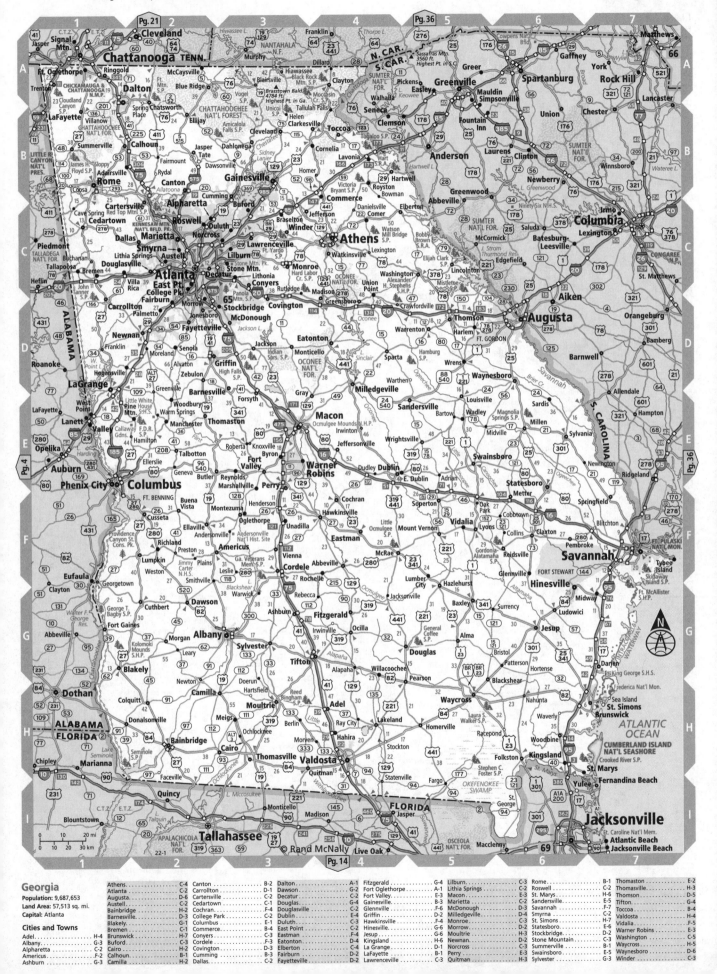

© Rand McNally

Georgia

Population: 9,687,653
Land Area: 57,513 sq. mi.
Capital: Atlanta

Cities and Towns

Adel H-4
Albany G-3
Alpharetta C-2
Americus F-2
Athens C-4
Atlanta C-2
Augusta D-6
Austell C-2
Bainbridge H-2
Barnesville D-3
Blakely G-1
Bremen C-1
Brunswick H-7
Buford B-3
Cairo H-2
Calhoun B-1
Camilla G-2
Canton B-2
Carrollton D-1
Cartersville B-2
Cedartown C-1
College Park C-2
Columbus E-1
Commerce B-4
Conyers C-3
Cordele F-3
Covington C-3
Cumming B-3
Dallas C-2
Dalton A-1
Dawson G-2
Decatur C-2
Douglas G-4
Douglasville C-2
Dublin E-4
Duluth C-3
East Point C-2
Eastman F-4
Eatonton D-3
Elberton C-5
Fairburn D-2
Fayetteville D-2
Fitzgerald G-4
Fort Oglethorpe A-1
Fort Valley E-3
Gainesville B-3
Griffin D-2
Hawkinsville F-4
Hinesville G-6
Jesup G-6
Kingsland H-6
La Grange D-1
Lawrenceville C-3
Lilburn C-3
Lithia Springs C-2
Macon E-3
Marietta C-2
McDonough D-3
Milledgeville D-4
Monroe C-3
Morrow C-2
Moultrie H-3
Newnan D-2
Norcross C-2
Perry E-3
Quitman H-3
Rome B-1
Roswell C-2
St. Marys H-6
Sandersville E-5
Savannah F-7
Smyrna C-2
St. Simons H-7
Statesboro E-6
Stockbridge D-2
Stone Mountain C-3
Summerville B-1
Swainsboro E-5
Sylvester G-3
Thomaston E-2
Thomasville H-3
Thomson D-5
Tifton G-4
Toccoa B-4
Valdosta H-4
Vidalia F-5
Warner Robins E-3
Washington C-5
Waycross H-5
Waynesboro D-6
Winder C-3

Idaho

Population: 1,567,582
Land Area: 82,643 sq. mi.
Capital: Boise

Cities and Towns

Aberdeen I-5
Albion I-5
American Falls I-5
Arco H-4
Ashton G-6
Athol B-1
Bancroft I-6
Bellevue H-3
Blackfoot H-5
Bliss I-3
Bloomington I-6
Boise H-2
Bonners Ferry A-2
Bovill D-2
Buhl I-3
Burley I-4
Caldwell H-1
Cambridge G-1
Carey H-4
Cascade G-2
Castleford I-3
Cataldo C-2
Challis G-3
Chester G-6
Clark Fork B-2
Coeur d'Alene C-1
Cottonwood E-2
Council F-1
Craigmont D-1
Culdesac D-1
Dayton J-5
Deary D-1
Declo I-4
Downey I-6
Driggs G-6
Dubois G-5
Eden I-3
Elk City E-2
Emmett G-1
Fairfield H-3
Fernwood C-2
Filer I-3
Firth H-5
Franklin J-6
Fruitland G-1
Georgetown I-6
Glenns Ferry I-3
Gooding I-3
Grace I-6
Grand View I-2
Grangeville E-2
Hagerman I-3
Hailey H-3
Hammett I-2
Hansen I-3
Harrison C-1
Hollister I-3
Homedale H-1
Horseshoe Bend G-2
Idaho City G-2
Idaho Falls H-5
Inkom I-5
Jerome I-3
Kamiah D-2
Kellogg C-2
Kendrick D-1
Ketchum H-3
Kimberly I-3
Kooskia E-2
Kootenai B-2
Lava Hot Springs I-5
Letha G-1
Lewiston D-1
Mackay G-4
Malad City J-5
Marsing H-1
McCall F-2
McCammon I-5
Melba H-1
Meridian H-1
Montpelier I-6
Moreland H-5
Moscow D-1
Mountain Home H-2
Moyie Springs A-2
Mud Lake G-5
Mullan C-2
Murphy H-1
Nampa H-1
Naples A-2
New Meadows F-2
New Plymouth G-1
Newdale G-6
Nezperce D-2
Oakley I-4
Orofino D-2
Osburn C-2
Paris I-6
Paul I-4
Payette G-1
Pierce D-2
Pinehurst C-2
Pleasantview I-5
Plummer C-1
Pocatello I-5
Post Falls C-1
Potlatch D-1
Preston J-6
Priest River B-1
Rathdrum B-1
Rexburg G-6
Richfield H-3
Rigby H-5
Riggins E-2
Ririe H-6
Roberts H-5
Rockland I-5
Rupert I-4
St. Anthony G-6
St. Maries C-1
Salmon F-4
Sandpoint B-1
Shelley H-5
Shoshone I-3
Silverton C-2
Soda Springs I-6
Spirit Lake B-1
Star H-1
Sugar City G-6
Sun Valley H-3
Swan Valley H-6
Sweet G-2
Tetonia G-6
Troy D-1
Twin Falls I-3
Victor H-6
Wallace C-2
Weippe D-2
Weiser G-1
Wendell I-3
Weston J-5

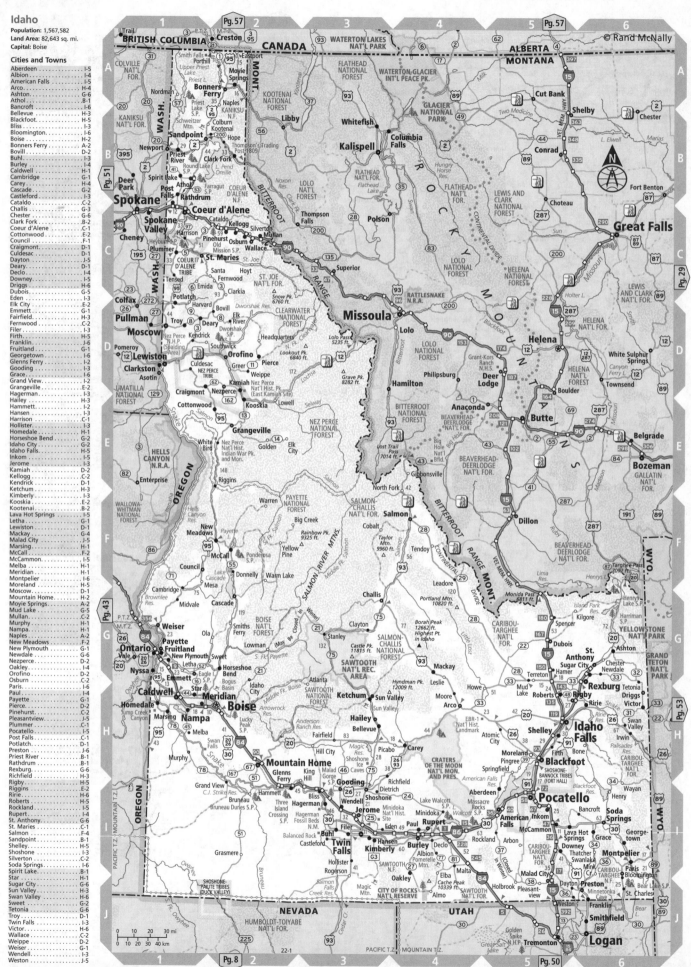

© Rand McNally

NOTE: Maps are not always in alphabetical order.
See Page 1 for map location in this atlas.

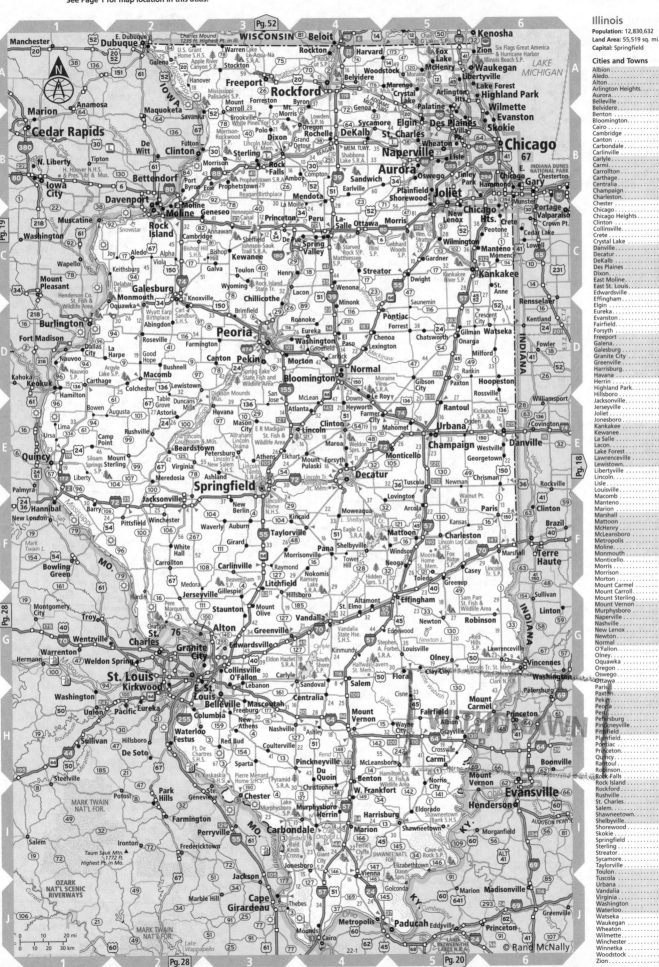

Illinois
Population: 12,830,632
Land Area: 55,519 sq. mi.
Capital: Springfield

Cities and Towns

Albion H-5
Aledo C-2
Alton G-3
Arlington Heights. . . . B-5
Aurora B-5
Belleville H-3
Belvidere A-4
Benton I-4
Bloomington. D-4
Cairo J-4
Cambridge C-3
Canton D-3
Carbondale I-4
Carlinville F-3
Carlyle G-3
Carmi. H-5
Carrollton F-2
Carthage D-1
Centralia H-4
Champaign E-5
Charleston F-5
Chester I-3
Chicago B-6
Chicago Heights C-6
Collinsville G-3
Crete C-6
Crystal Lake A-5
Danville E-6
Decatur E-4
DeKalb B-4
Des Plaines B-5
Dixon B-3
East Moline. C-2
East St. Louis G-3
Edwardsville G-3
Effingham G-4
Elgin B-5
Eureka D-4
Evanston B-6
Fairfield H-5
Forsyth E-4
Freeport A-3
Galena A-2
Galesburg C-2
Granite City G-3
Greenville G-3
Harrisburg. I-5
Havana E-3
Herrin I-4
Highland Park. A-6
Hillsboro G-3
Jacksonville F-2
Jerseyville G-2
Joliet B-5
Jonesboro I-4
Kankakee C-5
Kewanee C-3
La Salle C-4
Lacon. C-3
Lake Forest A-5
Lawrenceville G-6
Lewistown D-3
Libertyville A-5
Lincoln E-4
Lisle B-5
Louisville G-5
Macomb D-2
Manteno C-6
Marion I-4
Marshall F-6
Mattoon F-5
McHenry A-5
McLeansboro H-5
Metropolis J-4
Moline. C-2
Monmouth D-2
Monticello. E-5
Morris B-5
Morrison B-3
Morton D-3
Mount Carmel H-6
Mount Carroll B-3
Mount Sterling E-2
Mount Vernon H-4
Murphysboro I-4
Naperville B-5
Nashville H-4
New Lenox C-5
Newton G-5
Normal D-4
O'Fallon. G-3
Olney G-5
Oquawka C-2
Oregon B-4
Oswego B-5
Ottawa C-4
Paris F-6
Paxton D-5
Pekin. D-3
Peoria D-3
Peru C-4
Petersburg E-3
Pinckneyville H-4
Pittsfield F-2
Plainfield B-5
Pontiac D-4
Princeton C-3
Quincy E-1
Rantoul E-5
Robinson G-6
Rock Falls B-3
Rock Island C-2
Rockford A-4
Rushville E-2
St. Charles B-5
Salem. G-4
Shawneetown I-5
Shelbyville F-4
Shorewood C-5
Skokie B-6
Springfield E-3
Sterling B-3
Streator C-4
Sycamore B-4
Taylorville F-4
Toulon C-3
Tuscola F-5
Urbana E-5
Vandalia G-4
Virginia E-2
Washington D-3
Waterloo H-2
Watseka D-5
Waukegan A-5
Wheaton B-5
Wilmette B-6
Winchester F-2
Winnetka B-6
Woodstock A-5
Zion A-6

Indiana

Population: 6,483,802
Land Area: 35,826 sq. mi.
Capital: Indianapolis

Cities and Towns

Albion B-5
Alexandria D-5
Anderson E-5
Angola A-6
Attica D-2
Auburn B-6
Batesville G-6
Bedford H-3
Berne D-6
Bicknell H-2
Bloomfield G-3
Bloomington G-3
Bluffton C-6
Boonville I-2
Brazil F-2
Bremen B-4
Brookville F-6
Brownsburg E-4
Brownstown H-4
Carmel E-4
Cedar Lake B-2
Charlestown I-5
Chesterton A-2
Clarksville I-5
Clinton F-2
Columbia City B-5
Columbus G-4
Connersville F-6
Corydon I-4
Covington E-2
Crawfordsville E-3
Crown Point B-2
Danville F-3
Decatur C-6
Delphi D-3
DeMotte B-2
East Chicago A-2
Edinburgh G-4
Elkhart A-4
Elwood D-4
English I-3
Evansville J-1
Fort Wayne C-6
Fortville E-4
Fowler D-2
Frankfort F-4
Franklin F-4
French Lick H-3
Garrett B-6
Gary B-2
Gas City D-5
Goshen B-4
Greencastle F-3
Greenfield F-5
Greensburg G-5
Greenwood F-4
Hammond A-2
Hartford City D-5
Hebron B-2
Huntingburg I-3
Huntington C-5
Indianapolis F-4
Jasper I-3
Jeffersonville I-5
Kendallville B-5
Kentland C-2
Knox B-3
Kokomo D-4
Lafayette D-3
Lagrange A-5
La Porte A-3
Lawrenceburg G-6
Lebanon E-3
Liberty F-6
Ligonier B-5
Linton G-2
Logansport C-4
Lowell B-2
Madison H-5
Marion D-5
Martinsville F-3
Michigan City A-3
Mishawaka A-4
Mitchell H-3
Monticello C-3
Mooresville F-4
Mount Vernon J-1
Muncie E-5
Nappanee B-4
Nashville G-4
New Albany I-5
New Castle E-5
New Haven C-6
Newport E-2
Noblesville E-4
North Terre Haute F-2
North Vernon G-5
Paoli H-3
Pendleton E-5
Peru C-4
Petersburg H-2
Plainfield F-4
Plymouth B-4
Portage B-2
Portland D-6
Princeton I-1
Rensselaer C-2
Richmond E-6
Rising Sun G-6
Rochester C-4
Rockport J-2
Rockville F-2
Rushville F-5
Salem H-4
Schererville B-2
Scottsburg H-5
Sellersburg I-5
Seymour G-4
Shelbyville F-5
Shoals H-3
South Bend A-4
Spencer G-3
Sullivan G-2
Syracuse B-5
Tell City J-3
Terre Haute F-2
Tipton D-4
Union City E-6
Valparaiso B-2
Vernon G-5
Versailles H-6
Vevay H-6
Vincennes H-2
Wabash C-5
Warsaw B-4
Washington H-2
West Lafayette D-3
Westville A-3
Williamsport D-2
Winamac C-3
Winchester E-6

NOTE: Maps are not always in alphabetical order.
See Page 1 for map location in this atlas.

Iowa 19

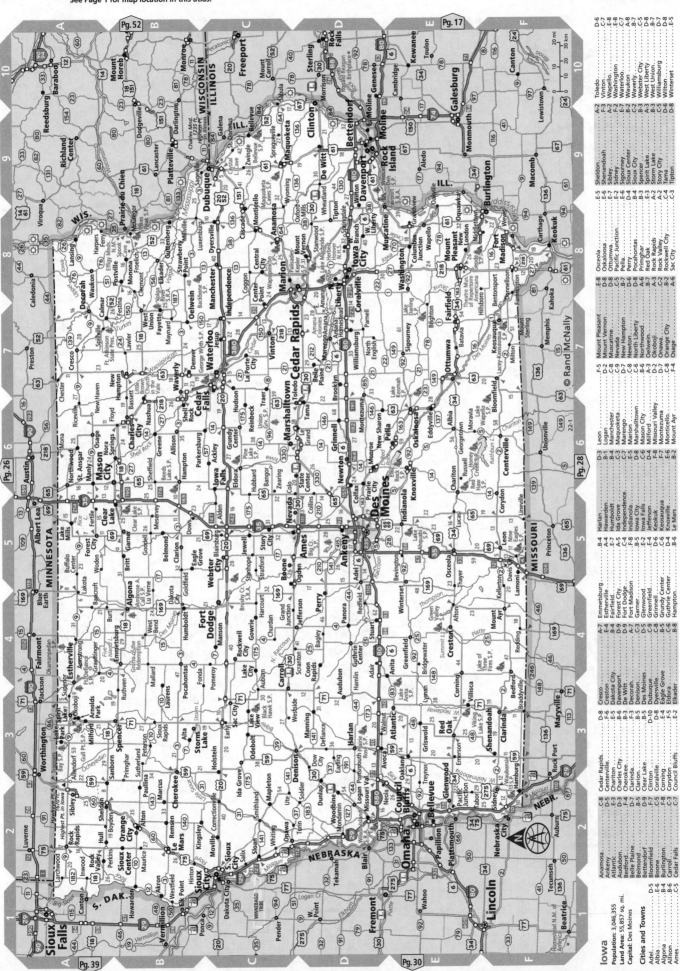

© Rand McNally

Iowa
Population: 3,046,355
Land Area: 55,857 sq. mi.
Capital: Des Moines

Cities and Towns

Adel D-5
Albia E-6
Algona B-4
Allison C-5
Ames D-5

Anamosa C-8
Ankeny D-5
Atlantic E-3
Audubon D-4
Belle Plaine D-7
Belmond B-5
Bettendorf D-9
Bloomfield F-7
Boone D-5
Burlington E-8
Carroll D-4
Cedar Falls C-5

Cedar Rapids C-8
Centerville D-5
Charles City B-3
Chariton E-6
Cherokee C-3
Clarinda F-3
Clarion B-5
Clear Lake B-5
Clinton D-9
Coralville C-8
Corning E-4
Corydon E-5
Council Bluffs E-2

Cresco A-7
Creston E-4
Dakota City B-4
Davenport D-9
De Witt D-9
Decorah A-7
Denison D-3
Des Moines D-5
Dubuque C-8
Dyersville C-8
Eagle Grove B-5
Eldora C-6
Elkader B-8

Emmetsburg A-4
Estherville A-4
Fairfield E-7
Fort Dodge C-4
Fort Madison E-8
Garner B-5
Glenwood E-2
Greenfield E-4
Grinnell D-6
Grundy Center C-6
Guthrie Center D-4
Hampton B-5

Harlan D-3
Hawarden B-2
Humboldt B-4
Ida Grove C-3
Independence C-7
Indianola E-5
Iowa City D-8
Iowa Falls C-6
Jefferson D-4
Keokuk F-8
Keosauqua F-7
Knoxville E-6
Le Mars B-2

Leon E-5
Logan D-3
Manchester C-7
Maquoketa C-9
Marengo D-7
Marion C-8
Marshalltown D-6
Mason City B-5
Milford A-3
Missouri Valley D-2
Monticello C-8
Mount Ayr F-4

Mount Pleasant ... E-8
Mount Vernon C-8
Muscatine D-8
Nevada D-5
New Hampton B-7
Newton D-6
North Liberty C-8
Northwood A-6
Oelwein C-7
Onawa D-2
Orange City B-2
Osage A-6

Osceola E-5
Oskaloosa E-6
Ottumwa E-6
Pacific Junction ... E-2
Pella E-6
Perry D-4
Pocahontas B-4
Primghar B-3
Red Oak E-3
Rock Rapids A-2
Rock Valley A-2
Sac City C-3

Sheldon B-3
Shenandoah F-2
Sibley A-3
Sidney F-2
Sigourney E-7
Sioux Center B-2
Sioux City C-2
Spencer B-3
Spirit Lake A-3
Storm Lake C-3
Story City C-5
Tama D-7
Tipton D-8

Toledo D-6
Vinton C-7
Wapello E-8
Washington E-8
Waterloo C-6
Waukon A-8
Waverly C-6
Webster City C-5
West Liberty D-8
West Union B-7
Williamsburg D-7
Wilton D-8
Winterset E-5

Pg. 17
Pg. 18
Pg. 28
Pg. 7
Pg. 27
Pg. 4

© Rand McNally

Kentucky

Population: 4,339,367
Land Area: 39,486 sq. mi.
Capital: Frankfort

Cities and Towns

Albany	F-9
Alexandria	A-10
Ashland	B-13
Barbourville	E-11
Bardstown	C-8

Beaver Dam	D-6
Benton	E-4
Berea	D-10
Bowling Green	E-7
Cadiz	E-5
Campbellsville	D-8
Carrollton	B-9
Central City	D-6
Columbia	E-9
Corbin	E-10
Cumberland	E-12
Cynthiana	B-10
Danville	D-9

Dawson Springs	E-5
Eddyville	E-4
Elizabethtown	D-8
Eminence	B-9
Falmouth	B-10
Flemingsburg	B-11
Florence	A-10
Fort Thomas	A-10
Frankfort	C-9
Franklin	F-7
Fulton	F-3
Georgetown	C-10
Glasgow	E-8

Greensburg	E-8
Greenville	E-6
Hardinsburg	C-7
Harlan	E-12
Harrodsburg	D-9
Hartford	D-6
Hazard	D-12
Henderson	C-5
Hickman	F-2
Hopkinsville	E-5
Horse Cave	E-8
Irvine	D-11
Jackson	D-11

Jeffersontown	C-8
Jenkins	E-13
La Grange	B-8
Lancaster	D-10
Lawrenceburg	C-9
Lebanon	D-9
Leitchfield	D-7
Lexington	C-10
London	E-11
Louisville	C-8
Madisonville	D-5
Marion	D-4
Mayfield	E-3

Middlesboro	F-11
Middletown	C-8
Monticello	E-9
Morehead	C-11
Morganfield	D-4
Morgantown	E-6
Mount Sterling	C-11
Mount Vernon	D-10
Mount Washington	C-8
Murray	F-4
Nicholasville	C-10
Owensboro	D-6
Paducah	E-3

Paintsville	C-12
Paris	C-10
Pikeville	D-13
Pineville	E-11
Prestonsburg	D-13
Princeton	E-4
Providence	D-5
Radcliff	C-8
Richmond	D-10
Russell Springs	E-9
Russellville	E-6
Scottsville	F-7
Shelbyville	C-9

Shepherdsville	C-8
Shively	C-8
Somerset	E-10
Springfield	D-9
Stanford	D-10
Stanton	C-11
Tompkinsville	F-8
Versailles	C-9
West Liberty	C-12
Williamsburg	F-10
Williamstown	B-10
Wilmore	C-10
Winchester	C-10

NOTE: Maps are not always in alphabetical order.
See Page 1 for map location in this atlas.

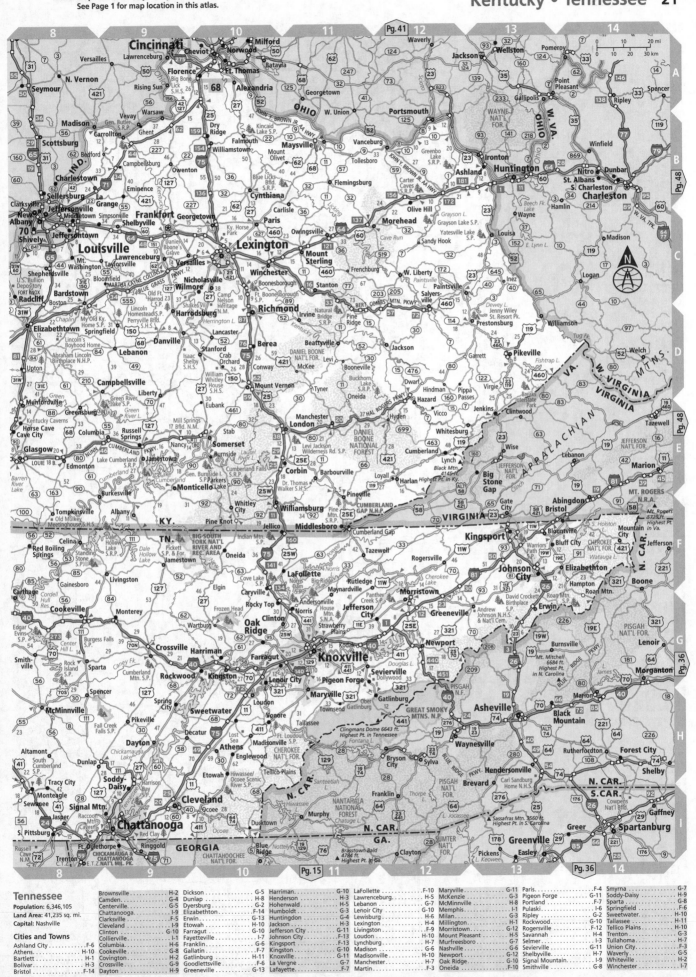

Tennessee

Population: 6,346,105
Land Area: 41,235 sq. mi.
Capital: Nashville

Cities and Towns

Ashland City F-6
Athens H-10
Bartlett H-1
Bolivar H-3
Bristol F-14
Brownsville H-2
Camden G-4
Centerville G-5
Chattanooga I-9
Clarksville F-5
Cleveland I-9
Clinton G-10
Collierville I-1
Columbia H-6
Cookeville G-8
Covington H-2
Crossville G-9
Dayton H-9
Dickson G-5
Dunlap H-8
Dyersburg G-2
Elizabethton F-14
Erwin F-13
Etowah H-10
Fayetteville I-7
Franklin G-6
Gallatin F-7
Gatlinburg H-11
Goodlettsville F-6
Greeneville G-13
Harriman G-10
Henderson H-3
Hendersonville F-6
Hohenwald H-5
Humboldt G-3
Huntingdon G-4
Jackson H-3
Jefferson City G-11
Johnson City F-13
Kingsport F-13
Kingston G-10
Knoxville G-11
La Vergne G-7
Lafayette F-7
LaFollette F-10
Lawrenceburg H-5
Lebanon G-7
Lenoir City G-10
Lewisburg H-6
Lexington H-4
Livingston F-9
Loudon H-7
Lynchburg H-7
Madison G-6
Madisonville H-10
Manchester H-7
Martin F-3
Maryville G-11
McKenzie F-4
McMinnville H-8
Memphis I-1
Millington H-1
Milan G-3
Morristown F-12
Mount Pleasant H-5
Murfreesboro G-7
Nashville G-6
Newport G-12
Oak Ridge G-10
Oneida F-10
Paris F-4
Pigeon Forge G-11
Portland F-7
Pulaski H-6
Ripley G-2
Rockwood G-10
Rogersville F-12
Savannah H-4
Selmer I-3
Sevierville G-11
Shelbyville H-7
Signal Mountain I-9
Smithville G-8
Smyrna G-7
Soddy-Daisy H-9
Sparta G-8
Springfield F-6
Sweetwater H-10
Tallassee H-11
Tellico Plains H-10
Trenton G-3
Tullahoma H-7
Union City F-3
Waverly G-5
Whiteville H-2
Winchester I-7

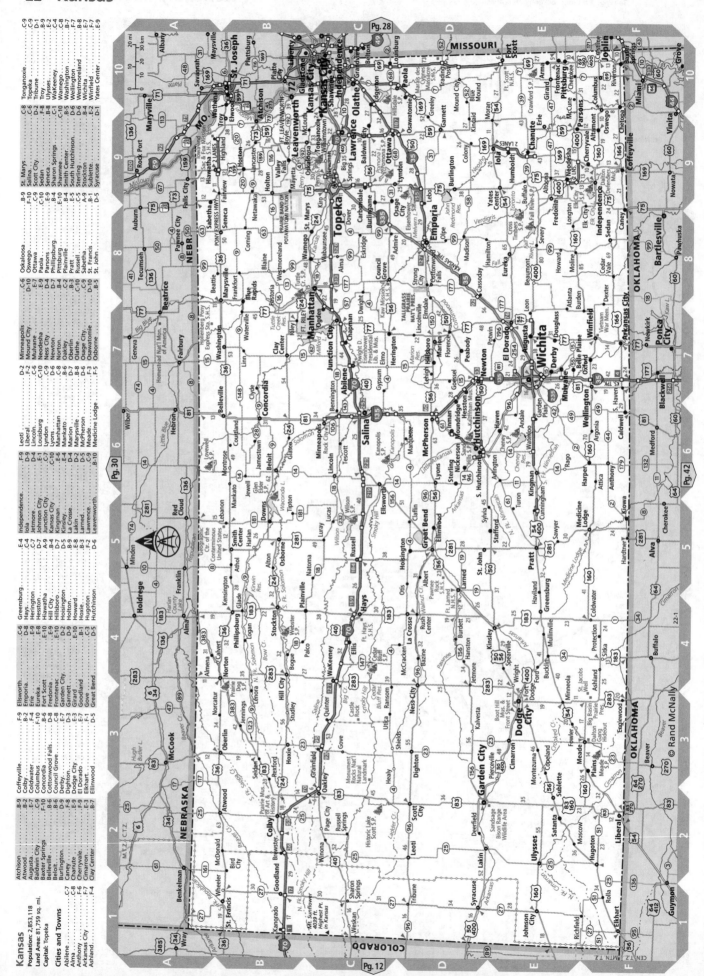

Kansas

Population: 2,853,118
Land Area: 81,759 sq. mi.
Capital: Topeka

Cities and Towns

Abilene C-7
Alma C-8
Anthony F-6
Arkansas City F-6
Ashland F-4

Atchison B-9
Atwood B-2
Augusta E-7
Baxter Springs F-10
Belleville B-6
Beloit B-6
Burlington D-9
Caney F-8
Chanute E-9
Cherryvale F-9
Cimarron E-3
Clay Center B-7

Coffeyville F-9
Colby B-2
Coldwater F-4
Columbus F-10
Concordia B-6
Cottonwood Falls .. D-8
Council Grove C-8
Derby E-7
Dighton D-3
Dodge City E-3
El Dorado E-7
Elkhart F-1
Ellinwood D-5

Ellsworth C-6
Emporia D-8
Erie E-9
Eureka E-8
Fort Scott D-10
Fredonia E-9
Frontenac E-10
Garden City E-2
Garnett D-9
Girard E-10
Goodland B-1
Gove C-3
Great Bend D-5

Greensburg E-4
Hays C-4
Herington C-7
Hesston D-6
Hiawatha B-9
Hill City C-3
Hillsboro D-7
Hoisington D-5
Holton B-8
Howard E-8
Hoxie B-3
Hugoton F-2
Hutchinson D-6

Independence F-9
Iola E-9
Jetmore D-4
Johnson City F-1
Junction City C-7
Kingman E-6
Kinsley E-4
Kiowa F-5
La Crosse D-4
Lakin E-2
Larned D-5
Lawrence C-9
Leavenworth C-9

Leoti D-2
Liberal F-2
Lincoln C-6
Louisburg C-10
Lyndon C-9
Lyons D-6
Manhattan B-8
Marion D-7
Marysville B-7
McPherson D-6
Meade F-3
Medicine Lodge ... F-5

Minneapolis C-6
Mound City D-10
Mulvane E-7
Ness City D-4
Newton D-7
Norton B-4
Oberlin B-3
Olathe C-10
Osage City C-8
Osawatomie D-10
Osborne C-5

Oskaloosa C-9
Ottawa D-9
Paola D-10
Parsons E-9
Pittsburg E-10
Plainville C-5
Pratt E-5
Russell C-5
Sabetha B-8
St. Francis B-1
St. John D-5

St. Marys C-8
Salina C-6
Scott City D-2
Sedan F-8
Seneca B-8
Sharon Springs ... C-1
Shawnee C-10
Stockton B-4
Sterling D-6
Stockton C-5
Sublette F-2
Syracuse D-1

Tonganoxie C-9
Topeka C-8
Tribune D-1
Troy B-9
Ulysses E-2
WaKeeney C-4
Wamego C-8
Washington B-7
Wellington E-6
Westmoreland B-8
Wichita E-7
Winfield E-7
Yates Center E-9

Pg. 28
Pg. 30
Pg. 12
Pg. 42

© Rand McNally

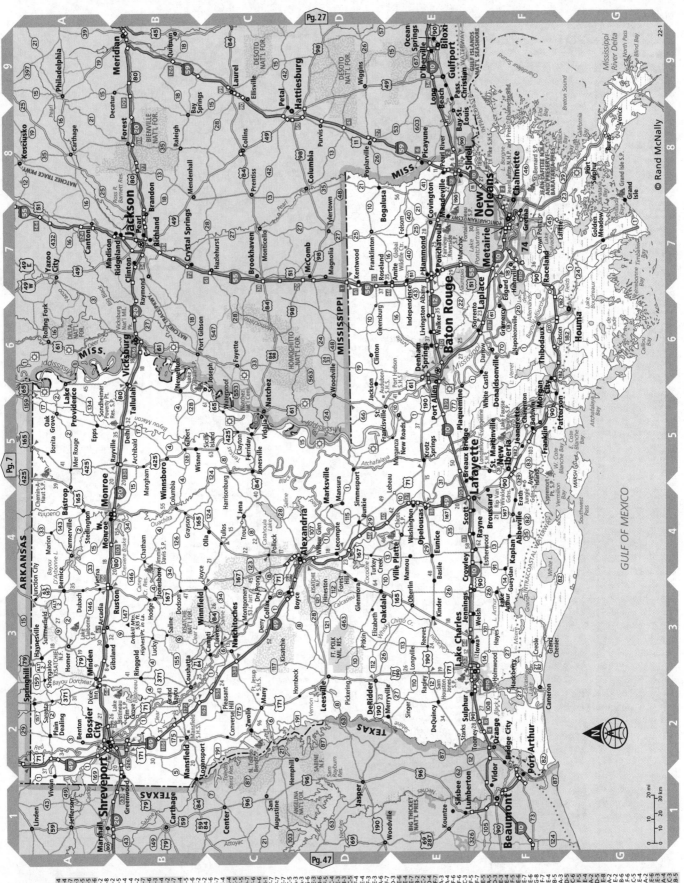

NOTE: Maps are not always in alphabetical order.
See Page 1 for map location in this atlas.

© Rand McNally

Louisiana

Population: 4,533,372
Land Area: 43,204 sq. mi.
Capital: Baton Rouge

Cities and Towns

Abbeville F-4
Alexandria D-4
Amite City E-7
Arcadia A-3
Baldwin F-5
Ball E-6
Baton Rouge E-6
Benton A-2
Bernice A-3
Bogalusa D-8
Bossier City A-2
Boyce D-4
Breaux Bridge F-4
Broussard F-4
Bunkie D-4
Cameron F-2
Chalmette E-7
Clinton D-6
Colfax D-4
Columbia C-3
Coushatta B-4
Covington E-7
Crowley F-4
Delhi B-5
Denham Springs E-6
DeQuincy F-2
DeRidder E-2
Donaldsonville F-6
Edgard F-7
Eunice E-4
Farmerville A-4
Ferriday C-5
Franklin F-5
Franklinton D-7
Gramercy F-6
Greensburg D-6
Greenwood A-2
Gretna F-7
Hahnville F-7
Hammond E-7
Harrisonburg C-5
Haynesville A-3
Homer A-3
Houma G-6
Iowa F-3
Jackson D-6
Jeanerette F-5
Jena C-4
Jennings F-3
Jonesboro B-4
Jonesville C-5
Kaplan F-4
Lafayette F-4
Lake Arthur F-3
Lake Charles F-3
Lake Providence ... A-5
Laplace F-7
Leesville D-2
Livingston E-6
Mamou E-4
Mandeville E-7
Mansfield B-2
Many C-2
Marksville D-4
Metairie E-7
Minden A-3
Monroe B-4
Morgan City F-6
Napoleonville F-6
Natchitoches C-3
New Iberia F-5
New Orleans E-7
New Roads E-6
Oak Grove A-5
Oakdale E-3
Oberlin E-3
Opelousas E-4
Patterson F-5
Plaquemine E-6
Ponchatoula E-7
Port Allen E-6
Port Sulphur G-8
Raceland F-6
Rayne F-4
Rayville B-5
Ruston A-3
St. Francisville .. D-6
St. Joseph C-5
St. Martinville ... F-5
Scott F-4
Shreveport A-2
Slidell E-7
Springhill A-2
Sulphur F-2
Tallulah B-6
Thibodaux F-6
Vidalia C-5
Ville Platte E-4
Vivian A-2
Walker E-6
Welsh F-3
West Monroe A-4
Winnfield C-3
Winnsboro B-5

Maine
Population: 1,328,361
Land Area: 30,843 sq. mi.
Capital: Augusta

Cities and Towns

Andover F-1
Ashland C-4
Auburn H-2
Augusta G-2
Bailey Island H-2
Bangor F-4
Bar Harbor G-5
Bath H-2
Belfast G-3
Bethel G-1
Biddeford I-1
Bingham F-2
Blue Hill G-4
Boothbay Harbor H-3
Brewer F-4
Bridgewater C-5
Bridgton H-1
Brownville Junction E-3
Brunswick H-2
Bucksport G-4
Calais E-6
Camden G-3
Caribou B-5
Castine G-4
Cherryfield G-5
Corinna F-3
Cornish H-1
Damariscotta H-3
Danforth D-5
Deer Isle G-4
Dexter F-3
Dixfield G-1
Dover-Foxcroft E-3
Eagle Lake B-4
East Corinth F-3
East Millinocket E-4
Eastport F-6
Ellsworth G-4
Fairfield G-2
Falmouth H-2
Farmington F-2
Fort Fairfield B-5
Fort Kent A-4
Freeport H-2
Friendship H-3
Fryeburg H-1
Gardiner G-2
Gorham H-1
Gray H-2
Greenville E-3
Guilford E-3
Hampden F-4
Harrington G-5
Harrison H-1
Houlton D-5
Howland E-4
Jackman E-2
Jonesport G-5
Kennebunk I-1
Kennebunkport I-1
Kingfield F-2
Kittery J-1
Lewiston H-2
Limestone B-5
Lincoln E-4
Livermore Falls G-2
Lubec F-6
Machias F-6
Madison F-2
Mars Hill C-5
Mattawamkeag E-4
Medway E-4
Mexico G-1
Milbridge G-5
Millinocket D-4
Milo E-4
Monson E-3
Monticello C-5
Naples H-1
Newport F-3
Norridgewock F-2
North Anson F-2
North Berwick I-1
North Bridgton H-1
North Windham H-2
Northeast Harbor G-4
Norway G-1
Ogunquit I-1
Old Orchard Beach I-1
Old Town F-4
Orono F-4
Patten D-4
Phillips F-2
Pittsfield F-3
Poland H-1
Port Clyde H-3
Portage B-4
Portland H-2
Presque Isle B-5
Princeton E-6
Rangeley F-1
Rockland H-3
Rockwood D-2
Rumford G-1
Saco I-1
Sanford I-1
Scarborough I-2
Searsport G-4
Sebago Lake H-1
Sherman Station D-4
Skowhegan F-2
Solon F-2
South China G-3
South Paris G-1
South Portland H-2
Southwest Harbor G-4
Standish H-1
Stonington G-4
Stratton E-1
Thomaston H-3
Turner G-2
Union G-3
Unity G-3
Van Buren A-5
Vinalhaven H-4
Waldoboro H-3
Washburn B-5
Waterville G-3
Wells I-1
West Enfield E-4
West Scarborough I-1
Westbrook H-2
Wilton G-2
Winslow G-3
Winterport F-4
Winthrop G-2
Woodland E-6
Yarmouth H-2
York Beach I-1
York Harbor I-1
York Village I-1

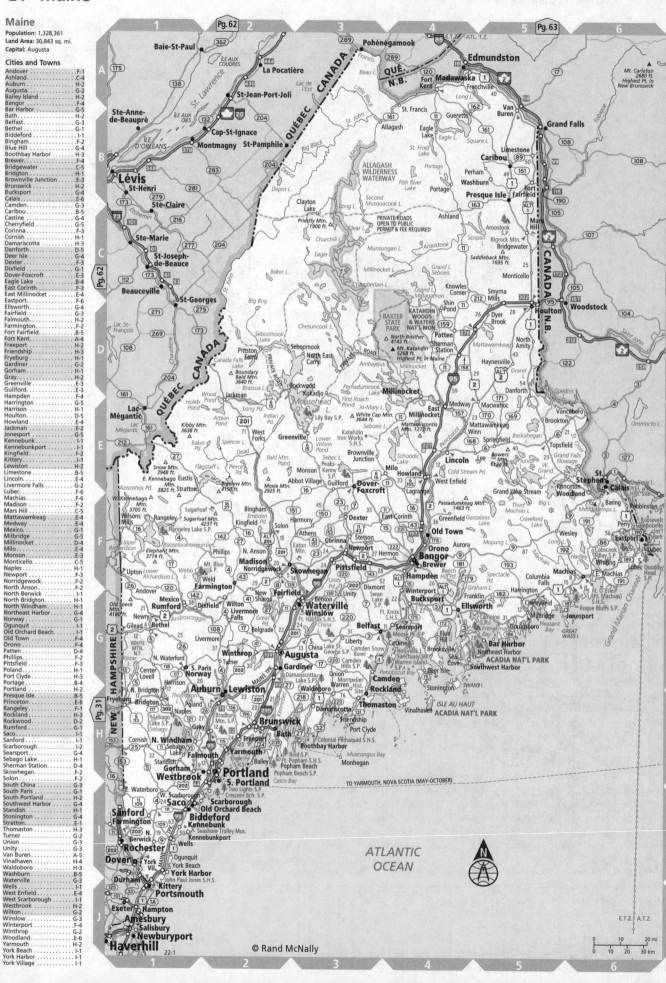

© Rand McNally

22-1

ATLANTIC OCEAN

NOTE: Maps are not always in alphabetical order.
See Page 1 for map location in this atlas.

© Rand McNally

© Rand McNally

Michigan
Population: 9,883,640
Land Area: 56,539 sq. mi.
Capital: Lansing

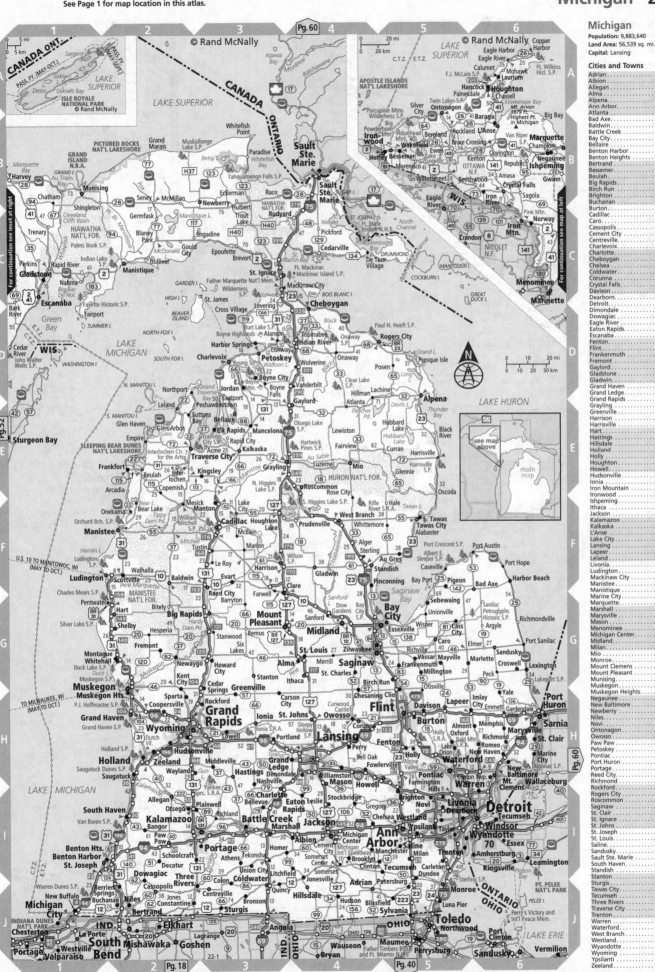

Cities and Towns

Adrian J-4
Albion I-4
Allegan I-2
Alma G-4
Alpena D-5
Ann Arbor I-5
Atlanta E-4
Bad Axe F-6
Baldwin F-3
Battle Creek I-3
Bay City G-4
Bellaire E-3
Benton Harbor I-2
Benton Heights I-2
Bertrand J-2
Bessemer B-5
Beulah E-2
Big Rapids G-3
Birch Run G-4
Brighton I-5
Buchanan J-2
Burton H-5
Cadillac F-3
Caro G-5
Cassopolis J-2
Cement City I-4
Centreville I-3
Charlevoix D-3
Charlotte I-4
Cheboygan D-4
Chelsea I-4
Coldwater J-3
Corunna H-4
Crystal Falls B-6
Davison H-5
Dearborn I-5
Detroit I-6
Dimondale H-4
Dowagiac J-2
Eagle River A-6
Eaton Rapids I-4
Escanaba C-1
Fenton H-5
Flint H-5
Frankenmuth G-5
Fremont G-2
Gaylord E-4
Gladstone C-1
Gladwin F-4
Grand Haven H-2
Grand Ledge H-4
Grand Rapids H-2
Grayling E-4
Greenville H-3
Harrison F-3
Harrisville E-5
Hart G-2
Hastings H-3
Hillsdale J-4
Holland H-2
Holly H-5
Houghton A-6
Howell H-5
Hudsonville H-2
Ionia H-3
Iron Mountain C-6
Ironwood B-5
Ishpeming B-6
Ithaca G-4
Jackson I-4
Kalamazoo I-3
Kalkaska E-3
L'Anse B-6
Lake City F-3
Lansing H-4
Lapeer H-5
Leland E-2
Livonia I-5
Ludington F-2
Mackinaw City C-3
Manistee F-2
Manistique C-2
Marine City H-6
Marquette B-6
Marshall I-3
Marysville H-6
Mason H-4
Menominee C-6
Michigan Center I-4
Midland G-4
Milan I-5
Mio E-4
Monroe J-5
Mount Clemens H-6
Mount Pleasant G-3
Munising B-1
Muskegon H-2
Muskegon Heights H-2
Negaunee B-6
New Baltimore H-6
Newberry B-3
Niles J-2
Novi I-5
Ontonagon B-5
Owosso H-4
Paw Paw I-2
Petoskey D-3
Pontiac H-5
Port Huron H-6
Portage I-3
Reed City F-3
Richmond H-6
Rockford H-3
Rogers City D-4
Roscommon E-4
Saginaw G-4
St. Clair H-6
St. Ignace C-3
St. Johns H-4
St. Joseph I-1
St. Louis G-4
Saline I-5
Sandusky G-6
Sault Ste. Marie B-4
South Haven I-2
Standish F-4
Stanton G-3
Sturgis J-3
Tawas City F-5
Tecumseh I-5
Three Rivers J-2
Traverse City E-2
Trenton I-5
Warren I-6
Waterford H-5
West Branch F-4
Westland I-5
Wyandotte I-5
Wyoming H-2
Ypsilanti I-5
Zeeland H-2

Minnesota
Population: 5,303,925
Land Area: 79,627 sq. mi.
Capital: St. Paul

Cities and Towns

Ada E-1
Aitkin F-4
Albert Lea J-4
Alexandria G-2
Anoka H-2
Appleton H-2
Austin J-5
Bagley D-2
Baudette C-3
Baxter F-3
Becker G-4
Belle Plaine H-4
Bemidji D-3
Benson G-2
Big Lake G-4
Blaine H-4
Bloomington H-4
Blue Earth J-3
Brainerd F-3
Breckenridge F-1
Buffalo H-4
Caledonia J-6
Cambridge G-4
Cannon Falls I-5
Chaska H-4
Chatfield J-5
Chisholm D-5
Cloquet E-5
Cohasset E-4
Cokato H-3
Crookston D-1
Crosby F-4
Delano H-4
Detroit Lakes E-2
Duluth E-5
East Grand Forks D-1
Eden Prairie H-4
Elbow Lake G-2
Elk River G-2
Ely D-6
Eveleth D-5
Fairmont J-3
Faribault I-4
Farmington H-4
Fergus Falls F-2
Foley G-4
Forest Lake H-5
Gaylord I-3
Glencoe H-3
Glenwood G-2
Grand Marais B-6
Grand Rapids E-4
Granite Falls H-2
Hallock C-1
Hastings H-5
Hibbing D-5
Hutchinson H-3
International Falls . . . C-4
Ivanhoe I-1
Jackson J-2
Jordan H-4
Kasson I-5
La Crescent J-6
Lake City I-5
Lake Crystal I-3
Lakeville H-4
Le Sueur I-4
Litchfield H-3
Little Falls G-3
Long Prairie G-3
Luverne J-1
Madelia I-3
Madison H-1
Mahnomen E-2
Mankato I-3
Marshall I-2
Milaca G-4
Minneapolis H-4
Montevideo H-2
Montgomery I-4
Monticello G-4
Moorhead E-1
Moose Lake F-5
Mora G-4
Morris G-2
New Prague I-4
New Ulm I-3
North Branch G-5
Northfield I-4
Olivia H-3
Ortonville G-1
Owatonna I-4
Park Rapids E-3
Paynesville G-3
Pelican Rapids F-2
Perham F-2
Pine City G-5
Pine Island I-5
Pipestone I-1
Plainview I-5
Preston J-6
Princeton G-4
Raymond H-2
Red Lake Falls D-1
Red Wing I-5
Redwood Falls I-3
Rochester I-5
Roseau B-2
St. Cloud G-3
St. James I-3
St. Joseph G-3
St. Paul H-5
St. Peter I-4
Sandstone F-5
Sauk Centre G-3
Sauk Rapids G-3
Shakopee H-4
Slayton I-2
Sleepy Eye I-3
Spring Valley J-5
Staples F-3
Stewartville J-5
Stillwater H-5
Thief River Falls C-1
Tracy I-2
Two Harbors E-6
Virginia D-5
Wabasha I-6
Wadena F-3
Walker E-3
Warren C-1
Waseca I-4
Wells J-4
Wheaton G-1
White Bear Lake H-5
Willmar H-3
Windom J-2
Winona I-6
Worthington J-2
Zimmerman G-4
Zumbrota I-5

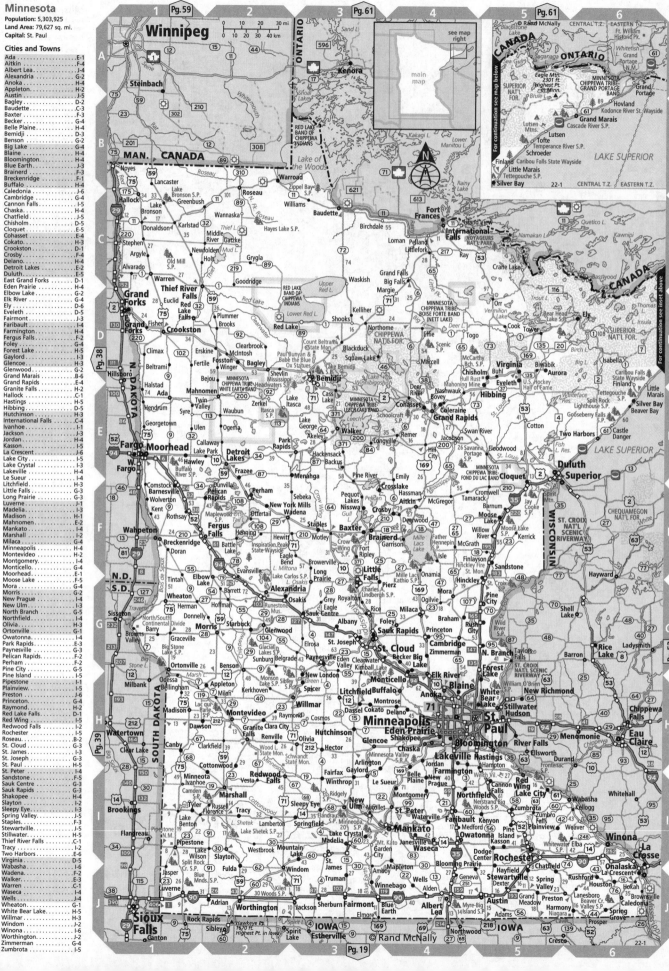

© Rand McNally

22-1

NOTE: Maps are not always in alphabetical order.
See Page 1 for map location in this atlas.

Mississippi 27

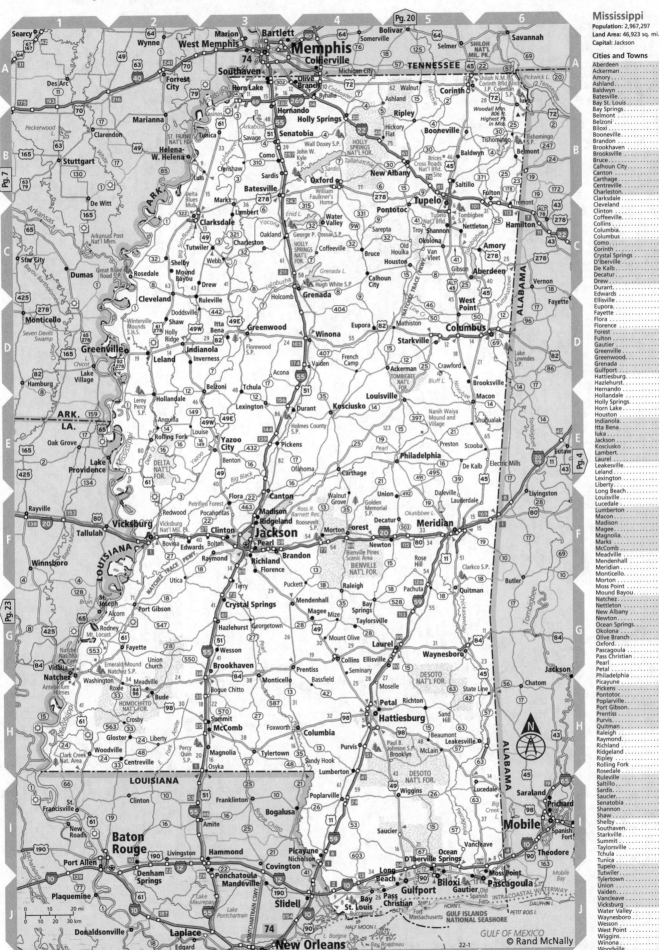

© Rand McNally

Mississippi
Population: 2,967,297
Land Area: 46,923 sq. mi.
Capital: Jackson

Cities and Towns

Aberdeen C-5
Ackerman D-5
Amory C-6
Ashland B-4
Baldwyn B-5
Batesville B-3
Bay St. Louis J-4
Bay Springs G-4
Belmont B-6
Belzoni D-3
Biloxi J-5
Booneville B-5
Brandon F-3
Brookhaven G-3
Brooksville D-5
Bruce C-4
Calhoun City C-4
Canton F-3
Carthage E-4
Centreville H-2
Charleston C-3
Clarksdale C-2
Cleveland C-2
Clinton F-3
Coffeeville C-4
Collins G-4
Columbia H-4
Columbus D-6
Como B-3
Corinth A-5
Crystal Springs G-3
D'Iberville I-5
De Kalb E-5
Decatur F-5
Drew C-2
Durant E-3
Edwards F-2
Ellisville G-5
Eupora D-4
Fayette G-2
Flora F-3
Florence F-3
Forest F-4
Fulton C-6
Gautier J-5
Greenville D-2
Greenwood D-3
Grenada C-4
Gulfport J-5
Hattiesburg H-4
Hazlehurst G-3
Hernando B-3
Hollandale E-2
Holly Springs A-3
Horn Lake A-3
Houston C-5
Indianola D-2
Itta Bena D-3
Iuka B-6
Jackson F-3
Kosciusko E-4
Lambert C-3
Laurel G-5
Leakesville H-6
Leland D-2
Lexington E-3
Liberty H-2
Long Beach J-5
Louisville E-5
Lucedale I-5
Lumberton H-4
Macon E-5
Madison F-3
Magee G-4
Magnolia H-3
Marks C-3
McComb H-3
Meadville H-2
Mendenhall G-3
Meridian F-5
Monticello G-3
Morton F-4
Moss Point J-6
Mound Bayou C-2
Natchez G-1
Nettleton C-5
New Albany B-4
Newton F-5
Ocean Springs J-5
Okolona C-5
Olive Branch A-4
Oxford B-4
Pascagoula J-6
Pass Christian J-4
Pearl F-3
Petal H-4
Philadelphia E-5
Picayune I-4
Pickens E-3
Pontotoc C-5
Poplarville I-4
Port Gibson G-2
Prentiss G-3
Purvis H-4
Quitman G-5
Raleigh G-4
Raymond F-3
Richland F-3
Ridgeland F-3
Ripley B-5
Rolling Fork F-2
Rosedale C-2
Ruleville C-2
Saltillo B-5
Sardis B-3
Saucier I-5
Senatobia B-3
Shannon C-5
Shaw C-2
Shelby C-2
Southaven A-3
Starkville D-5
Summit H-3
Taylorsville G-4
Tchula D-3
Tunica B-3
Tupelo C-5
Tutwiler C-3
Tylertown H-3
Union F-5
Vaiden D-4
Vancleave I-5
Vicksburg F-2
Water Valley C-4
Waynesboro G-5
Wesson G-3
West Point D-5
Wiggins I-5
Winona D-4
Woodville H-1
Yazoo City E-3

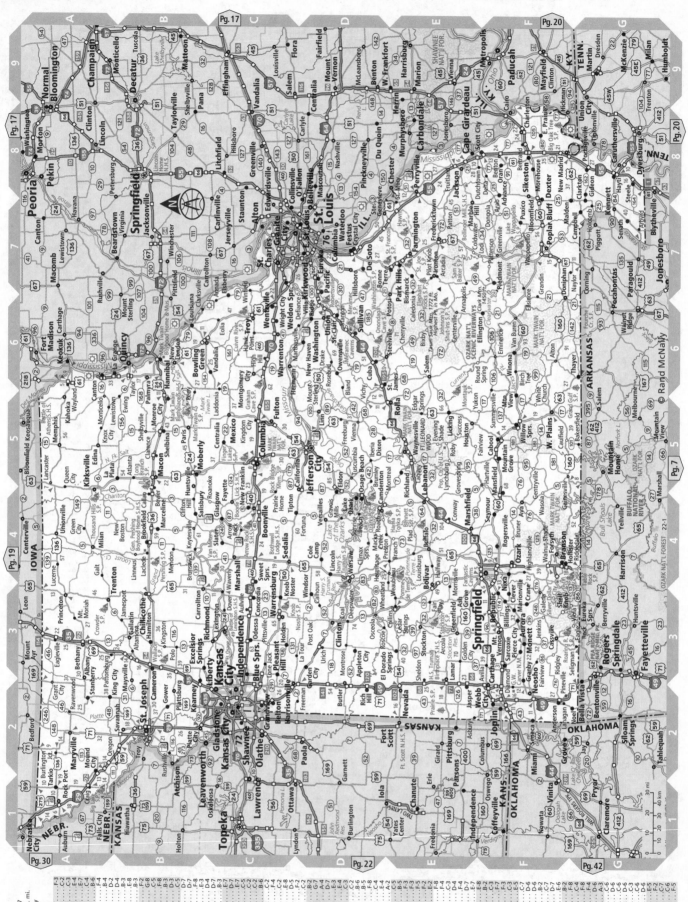

© Rand McNally

Missouri

Population: 5,988,927
Land Area: 68,741 sq. mi.
Capital: Jefferson City

Cities and Towns

Aurora F-3
Belton C-3
Blue Springs C-3
Bolivar E-4
Boonville C-4
Bowling Green B-6
Branson F-4
Brookfield B-4
Butler D-3
California C-5
Cape Girardeau ... E-8
Carrollton C-4
Carthage F-3
Caruthersville ... G-8
Centralia C-5
Charleston E-8
Chillicothe B-4
Clinton D-3
Columbia C-5
Crystal City C-7
De Soto C-7
Dexter E-8
El Dorado Springs E-3
Eureka C-6
Excelsior Springs C-3
Farmington D-7
Festus C-7
Fulton C-5
Fredericktown D-7
Gladstone C-3
Grandview C-3
Hannibal B-6
Harrisonville D-3
Hollister F-4
Independence C-3
Jackson E-8
Jefferson City ... C-5
Joplin F-3
Kansas City C-3
Kearney C-3
Kennett G-7
Kirksville A-5
Kirkwood C-7
Lamar E-3
Lebanon E-4
Lexington C-4
Liberty C-3
Louisiana B-6
Macon B-5
Malden F-8
Marshall C-4
Maryville A-2
Mexico C-5
Moberly B-5
Monett F-3
Mountain Grove ... E-5
Mount Vernon F-3
Nevada E-3
Nixa F-4
Odessa C-4
Osage Beach D-5
Ozark F-4
Park Hills D-7
Perryville D-7
Platte City C-3
Pleasant Hill D-3
Poplar Bluff F-7
Republic F-4
Richmond C-4
Rolla D-6
St. Charles C-6
St. Clair C-6
St. James D-6
St. Joseph B-3
St. Louis C-7
Ste. Genevieve ... D-7
Salem D-6
Sedalia C-4
Sikeston E-8
Springfield F-4
Sullivan C-6
Trenton B-4
Union C-6
Vandalia B-6
Villa Ridge C-6
Warrensburg D-4
Washington C-6
Waynesville E-5
Webb City F-3
Weldon Spring C-6
Wentzville C-6
West Plains F-5

Pg. 17
Pg. 20
Pg. 19
Pg. 7
Pg. 30
Pg. 22
Pg. 42

NOTE: Maps are not always in alphabetical order.
See Page 1 for map location in this atlas.

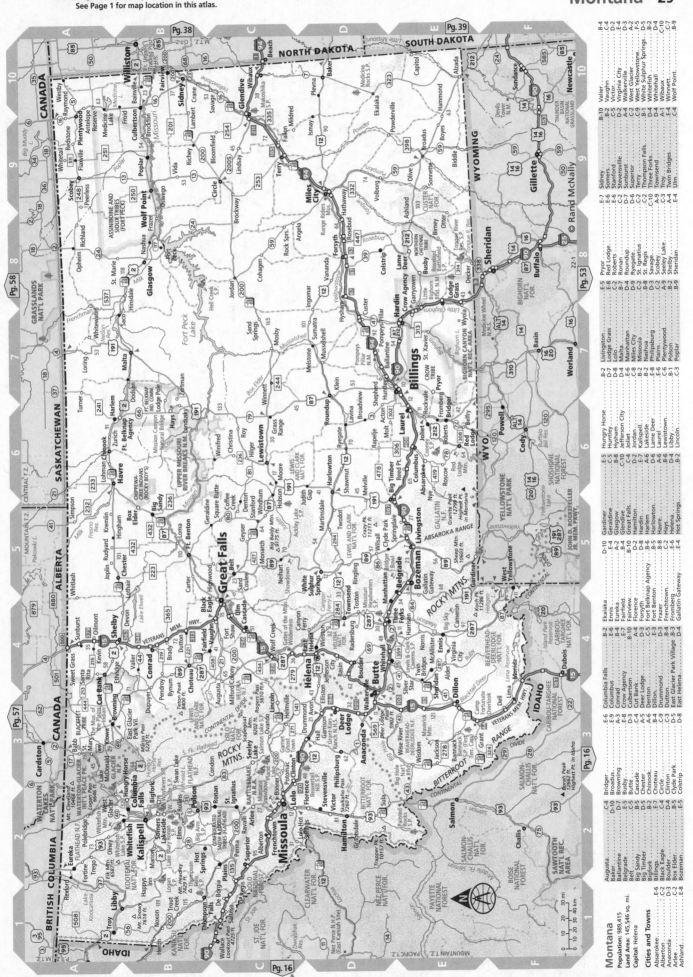

© Rand McNally

Montana

Population: 989,415
Land Area: 145,546 sq. mi.
Capital: Helena

Cities and Towns

Absarokee	E-6
Alberton	C-3
Anaconda	D-4
Arlee	C-3
Ashland	E-8
Augusta	E-6
Baker	D-10
Ballantine	E-7
Belgrade	D-5
Big Sandy	B-5
Big Timber	E-6
Bigfork	B-3
Billings	E-7
Black Eagle	D-5
Boulder	D-4
Box Elder	B-5
Bozeman	E-5
Bridger	C-4
Broadus	D-10
Browning	B-5
Busby	E-7
Cascade	D-4
Chester	B-5
Chinook	B-6
Choteau	C-4
Circle	D-9
Clinton	C-4
Clyde Park	D-5
Colstrip	E-8
Columbia Falls	E-6
Columbus	E-6
Conrad	B-4
Crow Agency	E-7
Culbertson	B-10
Cut Bank	C-4
Denton	C-6
Dillon	E-4
Drummond	C-4
Dutton	C-4
East Glacier Park Village	B-3
East Helena	D-4
Ekalaka	D-10
Ennis	E-5
Fairfield	C-4
Fairview	B-10
Florence	C-3
Forsyth	D-8
Fort Belknap Agency	B-6
Fort Benton	C-5
Frazer	B-8
Fromberg	E-6
Gallatin Gateway	E-5
Gardiner	D-10
Glasgow	A-8
Glendive	B-10
Great Falls	C-4
Hamilton	D-3
Hardin	E-7
Harlem	B-6
Harlowton	D-6
Havre	B-5
Helena	E-6
Hot Springs	B-2
Hungry Horse	E-5
Huntley	E-7
Hysham	B-8
Jefferson City	C-10
Joliet	C-4
Jordan	D-2
Kalispell	E-7
Lakeside	A-6
Lame Deer	D-6
Laurel	B-5
Lewistown	E-6
Libby	D-4
Lincoln	B-2
Livingston	B-2
Lodge Grass	D-7
Lolo	D-8
Malta	B-4
Manhattan	E-6
Miles City	C-8
Missoula	C-2
Nashua	A-6
Opheim	E-6
Philipsburg	D-3
Plains	B-2
Plentywood	B-1
Polson	D-4
Poplar	C-3
Pryor	E-5
Red Lodge	E-8
Roberts	B-7
Ronan	C-2
Roundup	D-6
Ryegate	D-9
St. Ignatius	C-8
St. Regis	C-2
Savage	D-3
Scobey	A-9
Seeley Lake	C-3
Shelby	C-6
Sheridan	B-9
Sidney	E-7
Somers	E-6
Stanford	C-2
Stevensville	D-6
Sunburst	A-4
Superior	A-2
Terry	C-9
Thompson Falls	C-2
Three Forks	D-5
Townsend	D-4
Troy	A-1
Twin Bridges	E-4
Ulm	C-4
Valier	B-4
Vaughn	C-4
Victor	D-2
Virginia City	E-5
Walkerville	A-4
West Yellowstone	A-2
White Sulphur Springs	D-5
Whitefish	B-1
Whitehall	D-4
Wibaux	C-10
Wolf Point	C-4

Valentine...............E-5
Valley.................D-9
Wahoo.................D-8
Wakefield.............C-8
Waverly...............D-8
Waverly...............D-8
Wayne.................C-8
West Point............C-8
Wilber................D-8
Wisner................C-8
Wood River............D-7
Wymore...............E-8
York.................D-8
Yutan.................D-9

Stockburg............B-9
Stromsburg...........D-8
Superior.............E-7
Sutherland...........D-4
Sutton...............D-8
Taylor...............C-8
Tecumseh.............D-8
Tekamah..............C-8
Thedford.............C-5
Tilden...............C-8
Trenton..............E-4
Tryon................C-5

Ponca................B-9
Ravenna..............D-7
Red Cloud............E-7
Rushville............B-3
St. Paul.............D-8
Schuyler.............D-8
Seward...............D-8
Sidney...............D-9
South Sioux City.....B-9
Stanton..............C-8
Stapleton............D-9

Loup City............D-7
Madison..............D-8
McCook...............E-5
Minatare.............D-6
Mitchell.............A-6
Mullen...............C-5
Nebraska City........D-9
Neligh...............D-1
Nelson...............E-8
Newman Grove.........D-8
Norfolk..............C-8
North Bend...........C-8
North Platte.........D-9

Hastings.............E-7
Hayes Center.........D-4
Hebron...............E-8
Hemingford...........B-3
Holdrege.............E-6
Hyannis..............C-4
Imperial.............D-5
Kearney..............D-7
Kimball..............D-1
Laurel...............C-7
Lexington............D-7
Lincoln..............D-8
Louisville...........B-8

Fullerton............D-8
Geneva...............E-8
Gering...............D-6
Gibbon...............D-8
Gordon...............A-3
Gothenburg...........D-5
Grand Island.........D-7
Grant................D-5
Greeley..............D-7
Harlisburg...........E-6
Hartington...........B-8

Cozad................B-5
Crawford.............C-2
Creighton............C-2
Crete................D-8
Dakota City..........C-6
David City...........D-6
Elwood...............D-5
Fairbury.............E-8
Franklin.............E-7
Friend...............D-8
Columbus.............C-9

Bloomfield...........C-3
Brewster.............D-9
Bridgeport...........B-6
Broken Bow...........D-7
Burwell..............C-7
Butte................B-6
Cambridge............E-5
Center...............C-7
Chadron..............E-5
Chappell.............D-9
Clay Center..........E-3
Columbus.............C-9

Arthur...............C-3
Ashland..............D-9
Atkinson.............B-6
Auburn...............E-10
Aurora...............D-7
Bartlett.............C-8
Bassett..............B-6
Bayard...............B-2
Beatrice.............E-8
Beaver City..........E-5
Bellevue.............B-2
Benkelman............E-6
Blair................E-5

Nebraska
Population: 1,826,341
Land Area: 76,824 sq. mi.
Capital: Lincoln

Cities and Towns
Ainsworth............B-5
Albion...............C-7
Alliance.............B-2
Alma.................E-6
Arapahoe.............E-5

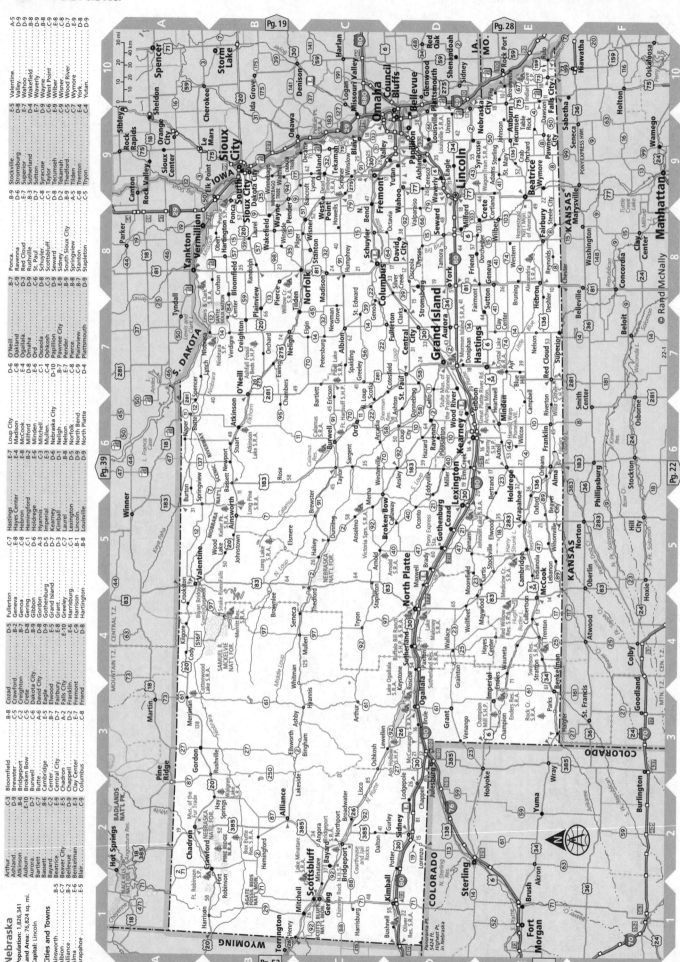

NOTE: Maps are not always in alphabetical order.
See Page 1 for map location in this atlas.

© Rand McNally

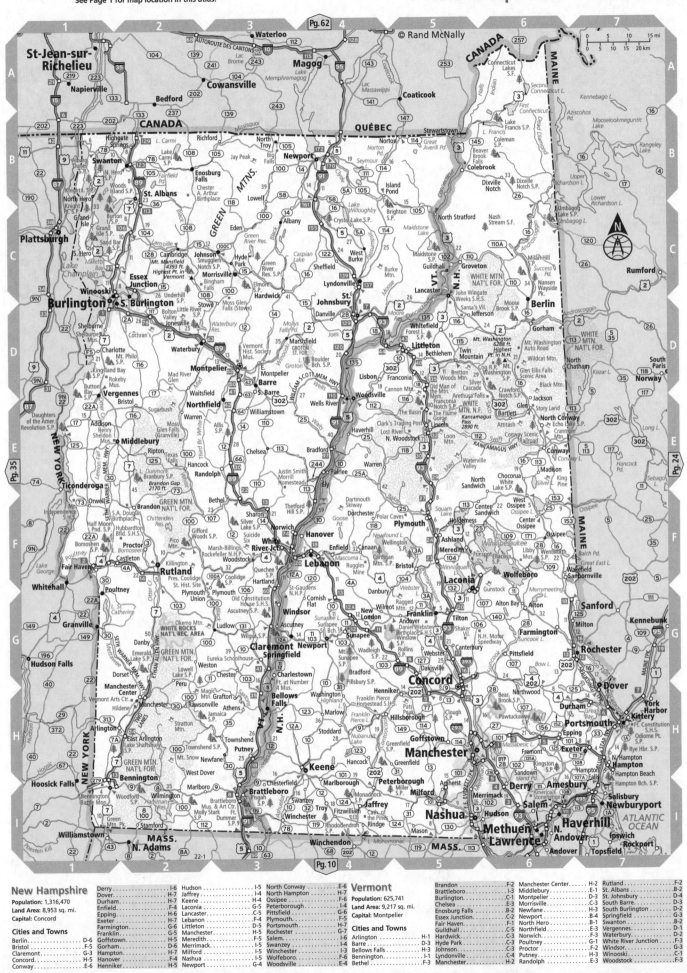

Pg. 62
Pg. 35
Pg. 24
Pg. 10

New Hampshire

Population: 1,316,470
Land Area: 8,953 sq. mi.
Capital: Concord

Cities and Towns

Berlin	D-6
Bristol	F-5
Claremont	G-3
Concord	H-5
Conway	E-6
Derry	I-6
Dover	H-7
Durham	H-7
Enfield	F-4
Epping	H-6
Exeter	H-6
Franklin	G-5
Goffstown	H-5
Gorham	D-6
Hampton	H-7
Hanover	F-4
Henniker	H-5
Hudson	I-5
Jaffrey	I-4
Keene	H-4
Laconia	G-5
Lancaster	C-5
Lebanon	F-4
Littleton	D-5
Manchester	H-5
Meredith	F-5
Merrimack	I-5
Milford	I-5
Nashua	I-5
Newport	G-4
North Conway	E-6
North Hampton	H-7
Ossipee	F-6
Peterborough	I-4
Pittsfield	G-6
Plymouth	F-5
Portsmouth	H-7
Rochester	G-7
Salem	I-6
Swanzey	I-4
Winchester	I-3
Wolfeboro	F-6
Woodsville	E-4

Vermont

Population: 625,741
Land Area: 9,217 sq. mi.
Capital: Montpelier

Cities and Towns

Arlington	H-1
Barre	D-3
Bellows Falls	H-3
Bennington	I-1
Bethel	F-3
Brandon	F-2
Brattleboro	I-3
Burlington	C-1
Chelsea	F-3
Enosburg Falls	B-2
Essex Junction	C-1
Fair Haven	F-1
Guildhall	C-5
Hardwick	C-3
Hyde Park	C-3
Johnson	C-3
Lyndonville	C-3
Manchester	H-2
Manchester Center	H-2
Middlebury	E-1
Montpelier	D-3
Morrisville	C-3
Newfane	H-3
Newport	B-4
North Hero	B-1
Northfield	E-3
Norwich	F-3
Poultney	G-1
Proctor	F-2
Putney	H-2
Randolph	E-3
Rutland	F-2
St. Albans	B-2
St. Johnsbury	D-4
South Barre	D-3
South Burlington	D-2
Springfield	G-3
Swanton	B-2
Vergennes	D-1
Waterbury	D-2
White River Junction	F-3
Windsor	G-3
Winooski	C-1
Woodstock	F-3

New Jersey

Population: 8,791,894
Land Area: 7,354 sq. mi.
Capital: Trenton

Cities and Towns

Absecon H-4
Asbury Park E-5
Atlantic City H-4
Atlantic Highlands . . . D-5
Audubon F-2
Avalon I-3
Beachwood F-5
Belleville C-5
Belvidere C-2
Berlin G-3
Bernardsville C-4
Blackwood G-2
Boonton C-4
Bordentown E-3
Bound Brook D-4
Bridgeton H-2
Brigantine H-4
Browns Mills F-4
Budd Lake C-3
Buena H-3
Burlington F-3
Caldwell C-5
Camden F-2
Cape May J-3
Cape May Court House . . J-3
Clifton C-5
Clinton D-3
Cranbury E-4
Denville C-4
Dover C-4
Eatontown E-5
Edison D-4
Egg Harbor City H-4
Elizabeth D-5
Elmer H-2
Ewing E-3
Flemington D-3
Folsom H-3
Forked River G-5
Franklin B-4
Freehold E-5
Glassboro G-2
Hackensack C-5
Hackettstown C-3
Hamburg B-4
Hammonton G-3
High Bridge D-3
Highland Park D-4
Highlands E-5
Hightstown E-4
Hopatcong B-4
Hope C-3
Hopewell E-3
Jamesburg E-4
Keansburg D-5
Kinnelon B-4
Lakehurst F-5
Lakewood F-5
Lambertville E-3
Lawrenceville E-3
Lebanon D-3
Linden D-5
Little Silver E-5
Long Branch E-6
Madison C-4
Mahwah B-5
Malaga H-2
Manahawkin G-5
Manville D-4
Margate City I-4
Marlton F-3
Matawan D-5
Mays Landing H-3
Medford F-3
Metuchen D-4
Middletown E-5
Millville H-2
Montclair C-5
Morris Plains C-4
Morristown C-4
Mount Holly F-3
Neptune City E-5
Netcong C-3
New Brunswick D-4
New Egypt F-4
New Providence C-4
Newark C-5
Newton B-3
Oakland B-5
Ocean City I-4
Ocean Grove E-5
Old Bridge D-4
Paramus B-5
Passaic C-5
Paterson C-5
Paulsboro G-2
Penns Grove G-1
Pennsville G-1
Perth Amboy D-5
Phillipsburg C-2
Piscataway D-4
Plainfield D-4
Pleasantville H-4
Point Pleasant F-5
Princeton E-4
Rahway D-5
Ramsey B-5
Raritan D-4
Red Bank E-5
Rio Grande J-3
Rochelle Park C-5
Salem H-1
Sayreville D-4
Scotch Plains D-4
Sea Girt F-5
Sea Isle City I-3
Seaside Heights F-5
Seaside Park F-5
Somerdale G-3
Somers Point I-4
Somerville D-4
South River D-4
Spring Lake Heights . . E-5
Sussex A-4
Toms River F-5
Trenton E-3
Tuckerton H-4
Union C-5
Ventnor City I-4
Villas J-3
Vineland H-2
Wanaque B-5
Washington C-3
West Milford B-4
West Orange C-5
Wildwood J-3
Williamstown G-3
Woodbury G-2
Woodstown G-2
Wyckoff B-5

© Rand McNally

22-1

NOTE: Maps are not always in alphabetical order.
See Page 1 for map location in this atlas.

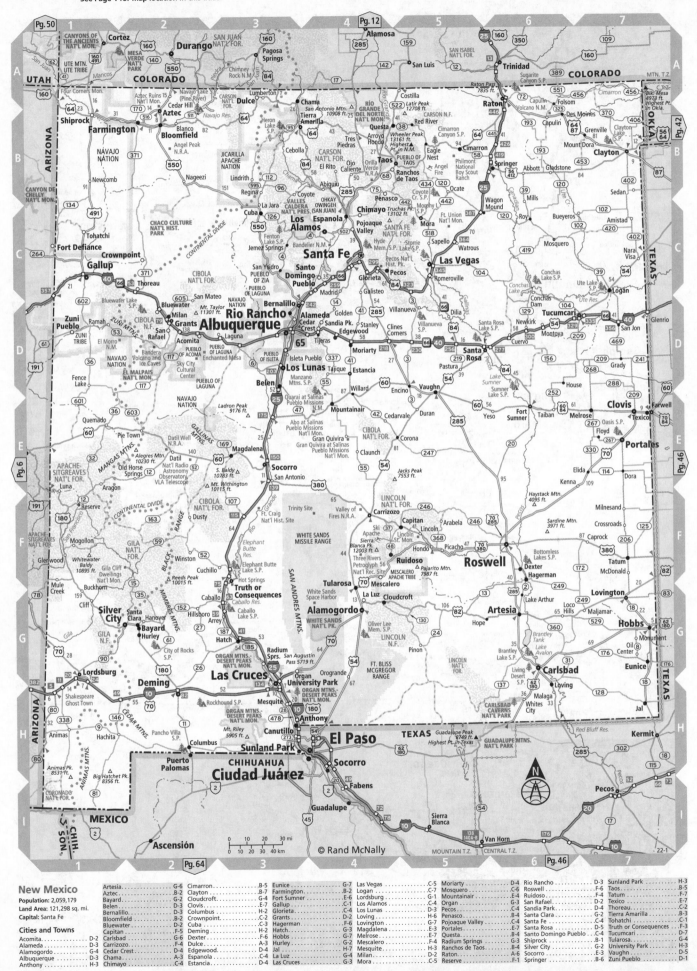

© Rand McNally

New Mexico

Population: 2,059,179
Land Area: 121,298 sq. mi.
Capital: Santa Fe

Cities and Towns

Acomita	D-2
Alameda	D-3
Alamogordo	G-4
Albuquerque	D-3
Anthony	H-3
Artesia	G-6
Aztec	B-2
Bayard	G-2
Belen	D-3
Bernalillo	D-3
Bloomfield	B-2
Bluewater	C-2
Capitan	F-5
Carlsbad	G-6
Carrizozo	F-4
Cedar Crest	D-4
Chama	A-3
Chimayo	C-4
Cimarron	B-5
Clayton	B-7
Cloudcroft	G-4
Clovis	D-7
Columbus	H-2
Crownpoint	C-2
Cuba	C-3
Deming	H-2
Dexter	F-6
Dulce	A-3
Edgewood	D-4
Espanola	C-4
Estancia	D-4
Eunice	G-7
Farmington	B-2
Fort Sumner	E-6
Gallup	C-1
Glorieta	C-4
Grants	D-2
Hagerman	F-6
Hatch	G-3
Hobbs	G-7
Hurley	G-2
Jal	H-7
La Luz	G-4
Las Cruces	G-3
Las Vegas	C-5
Logan	C-7
Lordsburg	G-1
Los Alamos	C-4
Los Lunas	D-3
Loving	H-6
Lovington	G-7
Magdalena	E-3
Melrose	E-7
Mescalero	F-4
Mesquite	H-3
Milan	D-2
Mora	C-5
Moriarty	D-4
Mosquero	C-6
Mountainair	E-4
Organ	G-3
Pecos	C-4
Penasco	B-4
Pojoaque Valley	C-4
Portales	E-7
Questa	B-4
Ranchos de Taos	B-4
Raton	A-6
Reserve	F-1
Rio Rancho	D-3
Roswell	F-6
Ruidoso	F-4
San Rafael	D-2
Sandia Park	D-4
Santa Clara	G-2
Santa Fe	C-4
Santa Rosa	D-5
Santo Domingo Pueblo	C-4
Shiprock	B-1
Silver City	G-2
Socorro	E-3
Springer	B-6
Sunland Park	H-3
Taos	B-4
Tatum	F-7
Texico	E-7
Thoreau	C-2
Tierra Amarilla	B-3
Tohatchi	C-1
Truth or Consequences	F-3
Tucumcari	D-7
Tularosa	G-4
University Park	G-3
Vaughn	D-5
Zuni Pueblo	D-1

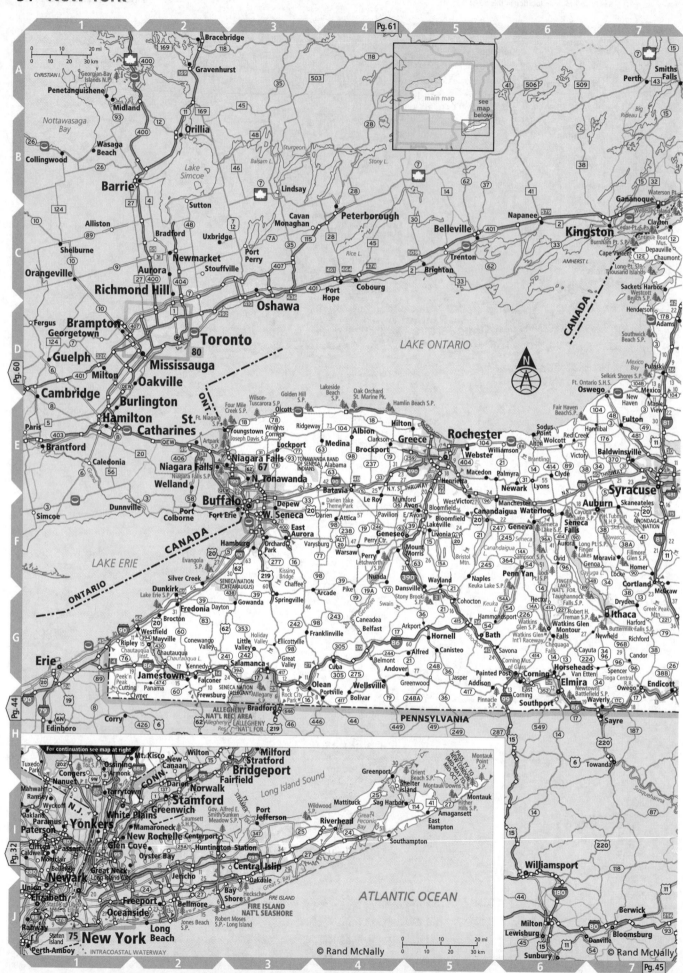

© Rand McNally

© Rand McNally

NOTE: Maps are not always in alphabetical order.
See Page 1 for map location in this atlas.

New York 35

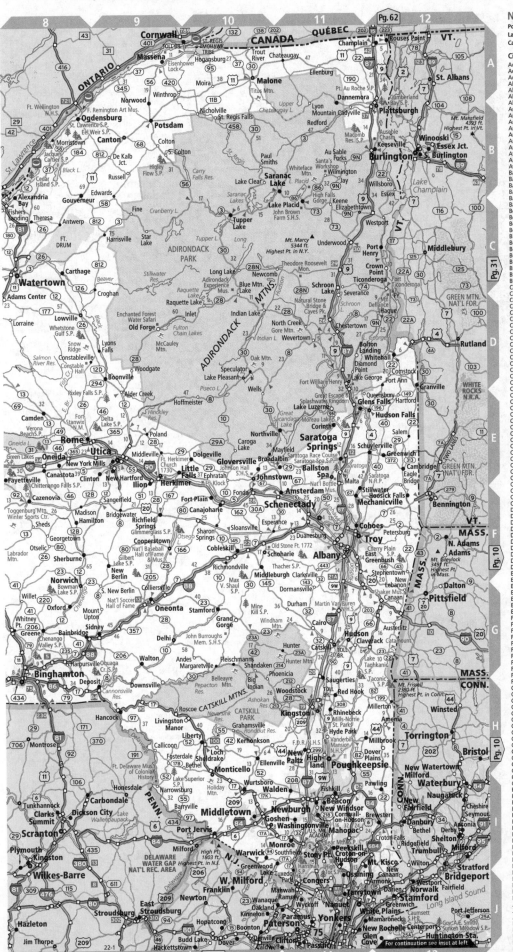

New York

Population: 19,378,102
Land Area: 47,126 sq. mi.
Capital: Albany

Cities and Towns

Adams D-7
Adams Center D-8
Addison G-5
Albany F-11
Albion E-4
Alexandria Bay B-8
Alfred G-5
Amagansett I-9
Amenia H-12
Amherst E-3
Amsterdam F-11
Andover G-5
Arcade F-3
Armonk J-11
Attica F-4
Auburn F-7
Avon F-5
Bainbridge G-8
Baldwinsville E-7
Ballston Spa E-11
Batavia E-4
Bath G-5
Bay Shore J-3
Beacon I-11
Belfast G-4
Bellmore J-2
Belmont G-4
Binghamton G-8
Bolivar H-4
Bolton Landing D-11
Boonville D-9
Brewster I-12
Brockport E-4
Brocton G-2
Buffalo F-3
Cadyville B-11
Cairo G-11
Cambridge E-12
Camden E-8
Canajoharie F-10
Canandaigua F-5
Canastota E-8
Candor G-7
Caniseo G-5
Canton B-9
Carthage C-8
Catskill G-11
Cayuta G-6
Cazenovia F-8
Centerport I-2
Central Islip I-3
Champlain A-12
Chestertown D-11
Claverack G-11
Clayton C-7
Clinton E-9
Clyde E-6
Cobleskill F-10
Cohocton G-5
Cohoes F-11
Congers H-1
Cooperstown F-9
Corinth E-11
Corning G-6
Cornwall-on-Hudson . . . I-11
Cortland F-7
Croton Falls I-12
Croton-on-Hudson I-11
Crown Point C-12
Cuba G-4
Dannemora A-11
Dansville F-5
Delhi G-9
Depew F-3
Deposit H-8
Dolgeville E-10
Dover Plains H-12
Downsville H-9
Dryden G-7
Dunkirk G-2
East Aurora F-3
East Greenbush F-11
East Hampton I-5
Elizabethtown C-11
Ellenville H-10
Elmira H-6
Endicott G-7
Falconer G-2
Fayetteville E-8
Fishkill I-11
Fonda F-10
Fort Ann D-12
Fort Plain F-10
Franklinville G-3
Fredonia G-2
Freeport J-2
Frewsburg H-2
Fulton E-7
Geneseo F-5
Geneva F-6
Glen Cove I-2
Glens Falls E-11
Gloversville E-10
Goshen I-10
Gouverneur B-8
Gowanda G-3
Grand Gorge G-10
Granville D-12
Great Neck I-1
Greece E-5
Greene G-8
Greenport H-4
Greenwich E-12
Greenwood Lake I-10
Hamburg F-3
Hamilton F-8
Hancock H-9
Henrietta E-5
Herkimer E-9
Highland H-11
Hilton E-5
Holcomb F-5
Homer F-7
Hoosick Falls F-12
Hornell G-5
Horseheads H-6
Hudson G-11
Hudson Falls E-12
Huntington Station I-2
Hyde Park H-11
Ilion E-9
Ithaca G-6
Jamestown G-2
Jericho I-2
Johnstown E-10
Keeseville B-11
Kerhonkson H-10
Kingston H-11
Lake George D-11
Lake Luzerne E-11
Lake Placid C-11

Lake Pleasant D-10
Lakeville F-5
Le Roy E-4
Liberty H-10
Little Falls E-9
Little Valley G-3
Livingston Manor H-9
Livonia F-5
Loch Sheldrake H-10
Lockport E-3
Long Beach J-2
Lowville D-8
Lyons E-6
Macedon E-5
Mahopac I-11
Malone A-10
Mamaroneck J-11
Manchester F-5
Massena A-9
Mattituck I-4
Mayville G-2
McGraw F-7
Mechanicville F-11
Medina E-4
Mexico D-7
Middleburgh F-10
Middletown I-10
Millbrook H-11
Millerton H-12
Monroe I-11
Montauk I-5
Monticello H-10
Montour Falls G-6
Moravia F-7
Mount Kisco I-11
Mount Morris F-4
Naples F-5
New Berlin F-9
New Hartford E-9
New Lebanon G-12
New Paltz H-11
New Rochelle J-11
New Windsor I-11
New York J-1
New York Mills E-9
Newark E-6
Newburgh I-11
Niagara Falls E-3
North Tonawanda E-3
Northville E-11
Norwich F-8
Norwood A-9
Nunda F-4
Oakdale I-3
Oceanside J-2
Ogdensburg B-8
Olcott E-4
Old Forge D-9
Olean H-3
Oneida E-8
Oneonta G-9
Orchard Park F-3
Ossining J-11
Oswego D-7
Owego G-7
Oxford G-8
Oyster Bay I-2
Painted Post G-6
Palmyra E-6
Pawling I-12
Peekskill I-11
Penn Yan F-6
Perry F-4
Plattsburg B-12
Port Henry C-12
Port Jefferson I-3
Port Jervis I-10
Portville H-4
Potsdam B-9
Poughkeepsie H-11
Pulaski D-7
Red Hook H-11
Rhinebeck H-11
Richfield Springs F-9
Ripley G-1
Riverhead I-4
Rochester E-5
Rome E-8
Rouses Point A-12
Sackets Harbor C-7
Sag Harbor I-5
St. Regis Falls B-10
Salamanca G-3
Salem E-12
Saranac Lake B-11
Saratoga Springs E-11
Saugerties G-11
Schenectady F-11
Schoharie F-10
Schroon Lake C-11
Schuylerville E-12
Seneca Falls F-6
Shelter Island I-4
Sherburne F-8
Sidney G-9
Silver Creek F-2
Skaneateles F-7
Sodus Point E-6
Southampton I-4
Southport H-6
Springville G-3
Stamford G-10
Star Lake C-9
Stillwater E-11
Stony Point I-11
Syracuse F-7
Tarrytown J-11
Ticonderoga C-12
Troy F-11
Tupper Lake C-10
Utica E-9
Varysburg F-4
Victor E-5
Walden I-11
Walton G-9
Warsaw F-4
Warwick I-10
Washingtonville I-11
Waterloo F-6
Watertown C-8
Watkins Glen G-6
Waverly H-7
Wayland F-5
Webster E-5
Wellsville G-4
West Seneca F-3
Westfield G-2
White Plains J-11
Whitehall D-12
Whitney Point G-7
Williamson E-6
Willsboro B-12
Wolcott E-6
Woodbury I-2
Woodstock H-11
Wurtsboro I-10
Yonkers J-11
Youngstown E-2

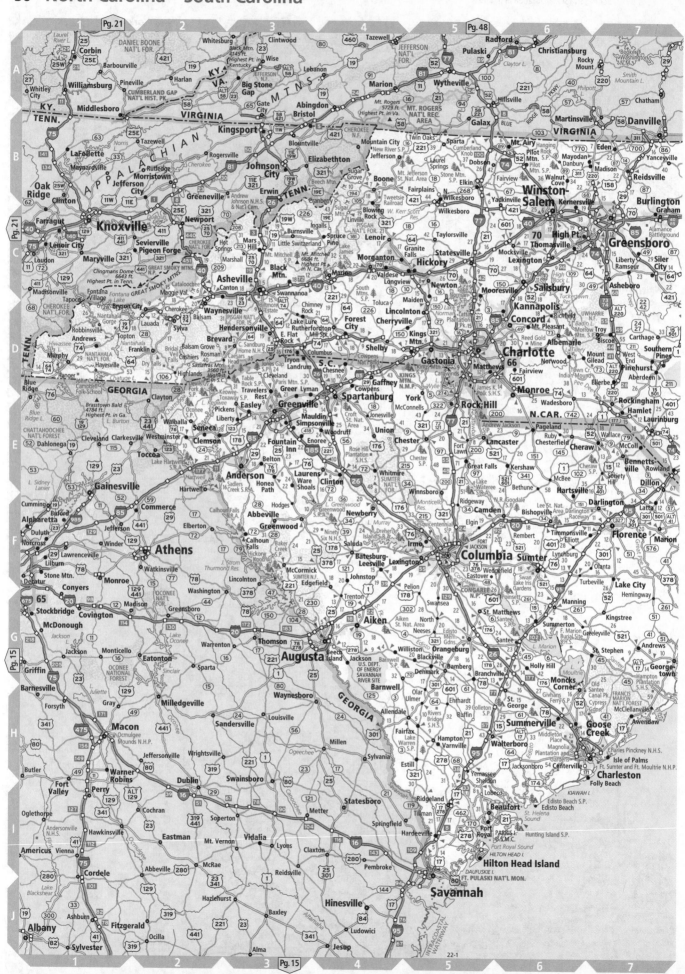

NOTE: Maps are not always in alphabetical order.
See Page 1 for map location in this atlas.

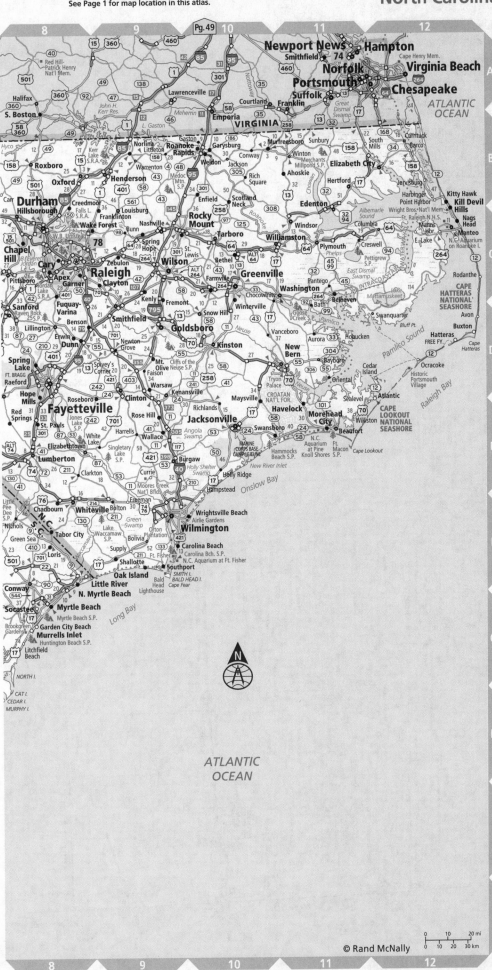

© Rand McNally

North Carolina
Population: 9,535,483
Land Area: 48,618 sq. mi.
Capital: Raleigh

Cities and Towns

Aberdeen D-7
Ahoskie B-11
Albemarle D-6
Apex C-8
Asheboro C-7
Asheville C-3
Bayboro D-11
Beaufort E-11
Benson D-8
Black Mountain C-3
Bolivia F-9
Boone B-4
Brevard D-2
Bryson City D-2
Burgaw E-9
Burlington C-7
Burnsville C-3
Canton C-2
Carolina Beach F-9
Carthage D-7
Cary C-8
Chapel Hill C-8
Charlotte D-5
Cherokee D-2
Cherryville D-5
Clayton C-8
Clinton D-9
Columbia C-12
Columbus D-3
Concord D-6
Currituck B-12
Danbury B-6
Dobson B-5
Dunn D-8
Durham C-8
East Flat Rock D-3
Eden B-6
Edenton C-11
Elizabeth City B-12
Elizabethtown E-8
Elkin B-5
Enfield B-10
Erwin D-8
Fairview D-6
Farmville C-10
Fayetteville D-8
Forest City D-4
Franklin D-2
Fuquay-Varina C-8
Garner C-8
Gastonia D-5
Goldsboro D-9
Graham C-7
Granite Falls C-4
Greensboro C-7
Greenville C-10
Hamlet E-7
Harbinger B-12
Havelock E-11
Hayesville D-1
Henderson B-9
Hendersonville D-3
Hertford B-11
Hickory C-5
High Point C-6
Hillsborough C-8
Hope Mills D-8
Jackson B-10
Jacksonville E-10
Jefferson B-4
Kannapolis D-6
Kenansville D-9
Kernersville B-6
Kill Devil Hills C-12
Kings Mountain D-5
Kinston D-10
Kitty Hawk B-12
Laurinburg E-7
Lenoir C-4
Lexington C-6
Liberty C-7
Lillington D-8
Lincolnton D-5
Longview C-5
Louisburg C-9
Lumberton E-8
Maiden C-5
Manteo C-12
Marion C-4
Marshall C-3
Matthews D-5
Mayodan B-6
Mocksville C-6
Monroe D-6
Mooresville C-5
Morehead City E-11
Morganton C-4
Mount Airy B-6
Mount Olive D-9
Murfreesboro B-10
Murphy D-1
Nags Head C-12
Nashville C-9
New Bern D-11
Newton C-5
North Wilkesboro B-5
Oak Island F-9
Oxford B-8
Pinehurst D-7
Pittsboro C-8
Plymouth C-11
Raeford D-8
Raleigh C-8
Red Springs E-8
Reidsville B-7
Roanoke Rapids B-10
Robbinsville D-1
Rockingham E-7
Rocky Mount C-9
Roxboro B-8
Rutherfordton D-4
Salisbury C-6
Sanford D-8
Scotland Neck B-10
Shallotte F-9
Shelby D-4
Siler City C-7
Smithfield D-9
Snow Hill D-10
Southern Pines D-7
Sparta B-5
Spring Lake D-8
Statesville C-5
Swannanoa C-3
Swanquarter D-12
Sylva D-2
Tabor City F-8
Tarboro C-10
Taylorsville C-5
Thomasville C-6
Troy D-7

Valdese C-4
Wadesboro D-6
Wake Forest C-9
Wallace E-9
Warrenton B-9
Warsaw D-9
Washington C-11
Waynesville D-2
Whiteville F-8
Wilkesboro B-5
Williamston C-11
Wilmington F-9
Wilson C-9
Windsor C-11
Winston-Salem C-6
Winterville C-10
Winton B-11
Wrightsville Beach F-10
Yadkinville B-6
Yanceyville B-7
Zebulon C-9

South Carolina
Population: 4,625,364
Land Area: 30,061 sq. mi.
Capital: Columbia

Cities and Towns

Abbeville F-3
Aiken G-4
Allendale H-5
Anderson E-3
Andrews G-7
Awendaw H-7
Bamberg G-5
Barnwell G-4
Batesburg-Leesville F-4
Beaufort I-5
Beech Island G-4
Belton E-3
Bennettsville E-7
Bishopville F-6
Blackville G-5
Branchville G-5
Calhoun Falls F-3
Camden F-6
Centerville H-6
Charleston H-7
Cheraw E-7
Chesnee D-4
Chester E-5
Chesterfield E-6
Clemson E-2
Clinton E-4
Columbia F-5
Conway F-8
Cowpens D-4
Darlington F-6
Denmark G-5
Dillon E-7
Easley E-3
Eastover F-5
Edgefield F-4
Elgin F-5
Enoree E-4
Estill H-5
Fairfax H-5
Florence F-7
Folly Beach H-7
Fort Lawn E-5
Fountain Inn E-3
Gaffney D-4
Garden City Beach G-8
Georgetown G-7
Goose Creek H-6
Great Falls E-5
Greenville E-3
Greenwood F-3
Greer D-3
Hampton H-5
Hardeeville I-5
Hartsville E-6
Hilton Head Island I-5
Holly Hill G-6
Honea Path E-3
Irmo F-5
Isle of Palms H-7
Jackson G-4
Johnston F-4
Jonesville E-4
Kershaw E-6
Kingstree G-7
Lake City F-7
Lancaster E-5
Landrum D-3
Latta F-7
Laurens E-4
Lexington F-5
Liberty E-3
Little River F-8
Loris F-8
Lyman D-3
Manning G-6
Marion F-7
Mauldin E-3
McBee E-6
McColl E-7
McCormick F-3
Moncks Corner G-6
Murrells Inlet G-8
Myrtle Beach F-8
Newberry F-4
North G-5
North Myrtle Beach F-8
Orangeburg G-5
Pageland E-6
Pickens E-3
Port Royal I-5
Ridgeland I-5
Rock Hill E-5
St. George H-6
St. Matthews G-5
St. Stephen G-7
Saluda F-4
Santee G-6
Seneca E-2
Simpsonville E-3
Socastee G-8
Society Hill E-7
Spartanburg D-4
Summerton G-6
Summerville H-6
Sumter F-6
Timmonsville F-7
Travelers Rest D-3
Turbeville F-6
Union E-4
Varnville H-5
Walhalla E-2
Walterboro H-5
Ware Shoals E-3
Westminster E-2
Whitmire E-4
Williston G-4
Winnsboro E-5
Woodruff E-4
Yemassee H-5
York D-5

North Dakota

Population: 672,591
Land Area: 69,000 sq. mi.
Capital: Bismarck

Cities and Towns

Abercrombie	E-10
Amidon	E-2
Anamoose	C-6
Aneta	C-8
Arthur	D-9

Ashley	F-7
Beach	D-1
Belcourt	A-6
Beulah	D-4
Bismarck	D-5
Bowbells	A-3
Bowman	E-2
Burlington	B-4
Cando	B-7
Cannon Ball	D-5

Carrington	C-7
Carson	D-4
Casselton	D-9
Cavalier	A-9
Center	D-4
Cooperstown	C-8
Crosby	A-2
Devils Lake	B-7
Dickinson	D-3
Drake	C-6
Drayton	A-9
Dunseith	A-6
Edgeley	E-7

Elgin	C-7
Ellendale	E-4
Enderlin	D-9
Fairmount	F-10
Fessenden	C-8
Finley	C-8
Flasher	D-3
Fort Totten	C-6
Fort Yates	E-7
Garrison	C-6

Glen Ullin	E-4
Glenburn	B-5
Grafton	A-9
Grand Forks	B-9
Gwinner	D-9
Harvey	C-6
Hatton	C-9
Hazelton	E-6
Hebron	D-4
Hettinger	E-3
Hillsboro	C-9

Hope	C-8
Hunter	D-9
Jamestown	D-7
Kenmare	B-4
Killdeer	C-3
Kindred	D-9
Kulm	E-7
Lakota	B-8
Langdon	A-8
Larimore	B-9
Leeds	B-7
Lidgerwood	E-9

Lincoln	D-5
Linton	E-6
Lisbon	D-9
Maddock	C-6
Mandan	D-5
Mandaree	C-3
Manning	D-3
Manvel	B-9
Max	C-5
Mayville	C-9
McClusky	C-6
McVille	C-8
Medina	D-7

Medora	E-2
Michigan	C-8
Minnewaukan	B-6
Minot	C-5
Minto	B-9
Mohall	A-4
Mott	E-3
Napoleon	E-6
Neche	A-9
New England	E-3
New Rockford	C-7

New Salem	D-4
New Town	C-3
Northwood	C-9
Oakes	E-8
Park River	B-9
Parshall	B-4
Pembina	A-9
Powers Lake	B-3
Ray	B-2
Richardton	D-3
Rolette	A-6
Rolla	A-6
Rugby	B-6

St. Thomas	A-9
Scranton	E-2
Sheyenne	C-7
Stanton	C-4
Steele	D-6
Strasburg	E-6
Surrey	C-5
Thompson	B-9
Tioga	B-3
Tower City	D-8
Turtle Lake	C-5
Underwood	C-5

Valley City	D-8
Velva	B-5
Wahpeton	E-10
Walhalla	A-8
Washburn	D-5
West Fargo	D-10
Westhope	A-5
Williston	B-2
Wilton	D-5
Wishek	E-6
Wyndmere	E-9

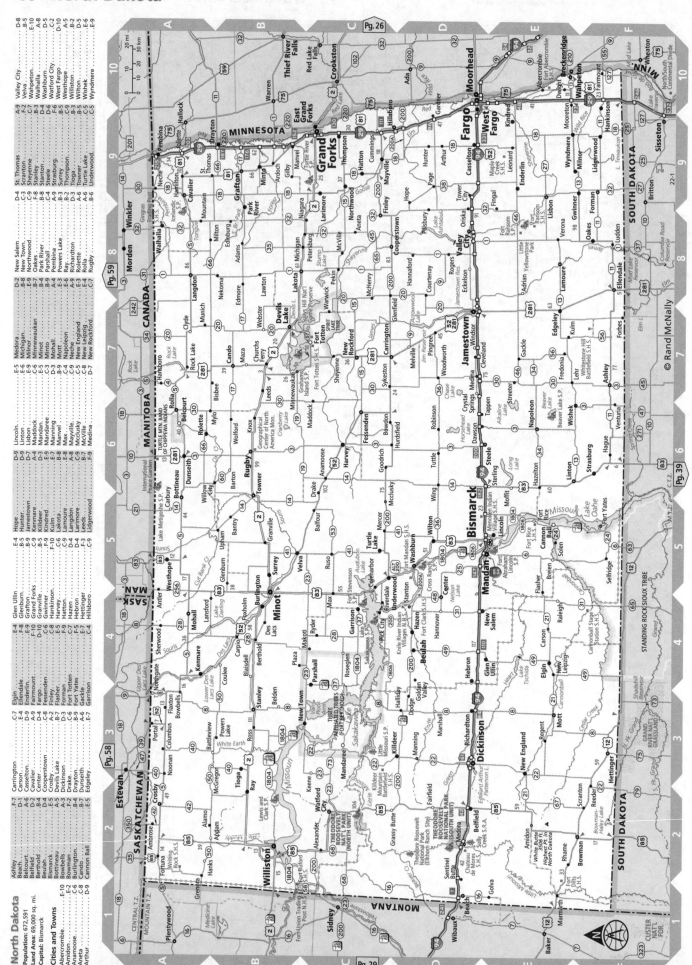

NOTE: Maps are not always in alphabetical order.
See Page 1 for map location in this atlas.

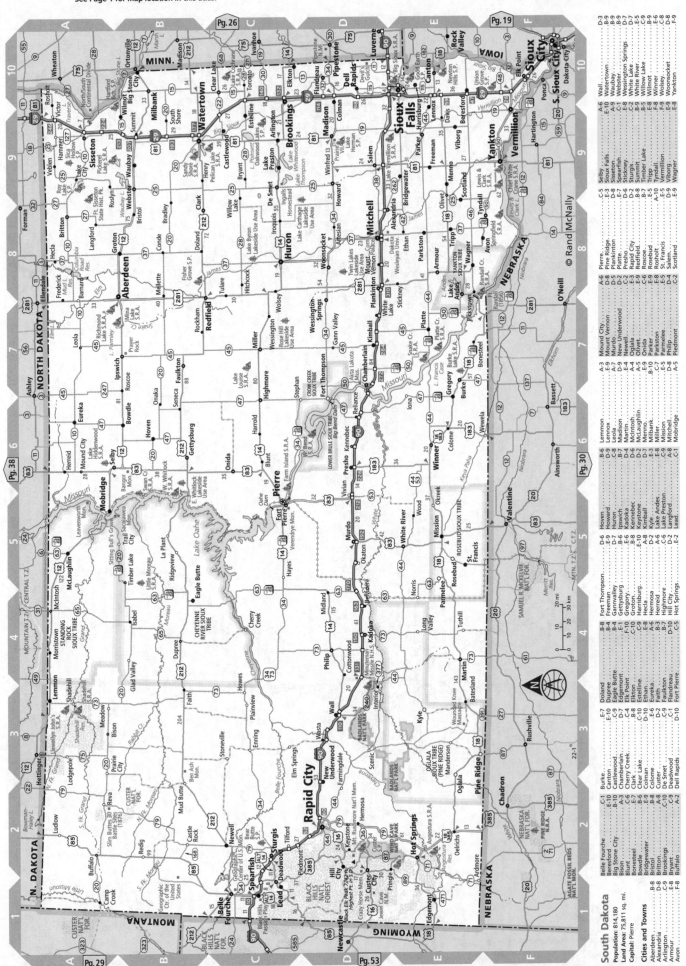

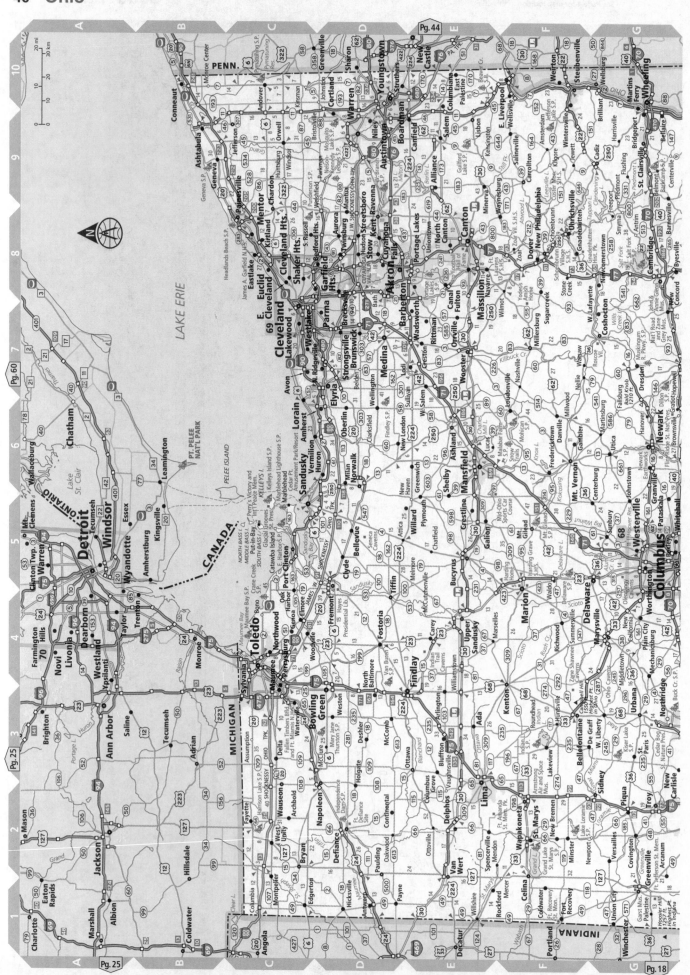

NOTE: Maps are not always in alphabetical order.
See Page 1 for map location in this atlas.

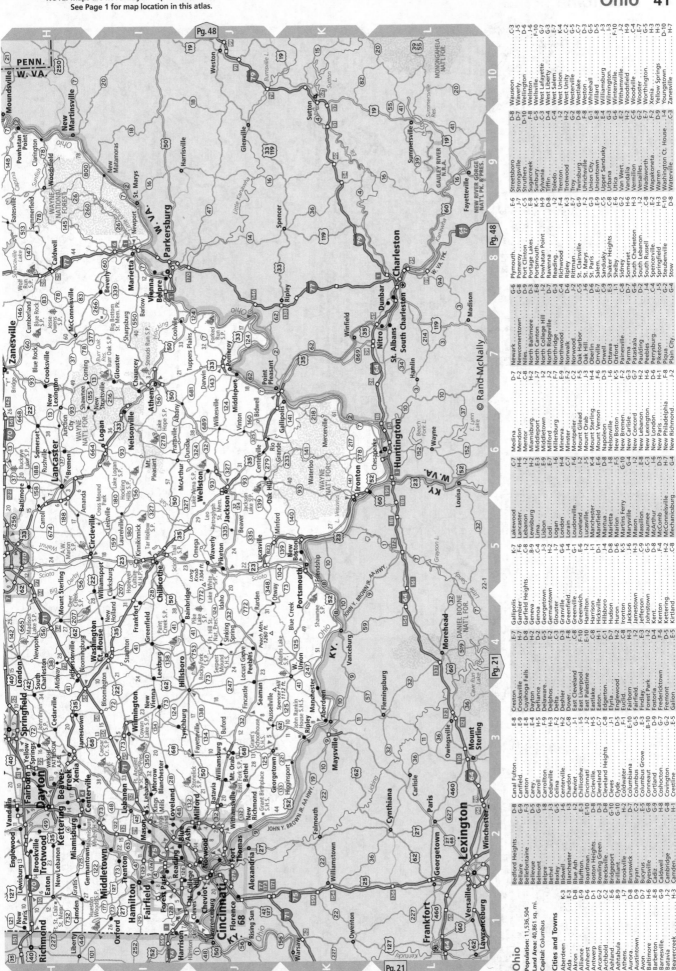

© Rand McNally

Oklahoma
Population: 3,751,351
Land Area: 68,595 sq. mi.
Capital: Oklahoma City

Cities and Towns

Ada...D-8
Altus...D-5
Alva...A-5
Anadarko...C-6
Antlers...E-9
Apache...C-6
Arapaho...C-5
Arnett...B-4
Atoka...D-8
Bartlesville...A-8
Beaver...A-4
Bixby...B-9
Blackwell...B-7
Blanchard...C-7
Boise City...A-2
Bristow...B-8
Broken Arrow...B-9
Broken Bow...D-10
Buffalo...A-4
Calera...D-8
Carnegie...C-6
Chandler...C-7
Checotah...C-9
Chelsea...A-9
Cherokee...A-5
Cheyenne...B-4
Chickasha...C-7
Chouteau...B-9
Claremore...B-9
Cleveland...C-7
Clinton...C-5
Collinsville...B-8
Commerce...A-10
Cordell...C-5
Coweta...B-9
Cushing...B-8
Davis...D-7
Dewey...A-8
Drumright...B-8
Durant...D-8
Edmond...C-7
El Reno...C-6
Elk City...C-4
Enid...B-6
Eufaula...C-9
Fairview...B-5
Frederick...D-6
Grove...A-10
Guthrie...C-7
Guymon...A-2
Haskell...B-9
Healdton...D-6
Heavener...C-10
Hennessey...B-6
Hinton...C-6
Hobart...C-5
Holdenville...C-8
Hollis...D-4
Hominy...B-8
Hooker...A-3
Hugo...E-9
Idabel...E-10
Jay...B-10
Kingfisher...C-6
Krebs...C-9
Lawton...D-6
Lone Grove...D-7
Madill...D-8
Mangum...D-4
Marietta...E-7
McAlester...C-9
Medford...B-6
Miami...A-10
Midwest City...C-7
Minco...C-6
Moore...C-7
Muskogee...C-9
Newkirk...A-7
Norman...C-7
Nowata...A-9
Okemah...C-8
Okmulgee...C-9
Oologah...A-8
Pauls Valley...C-7
Pawhuska...B-8
Pawnee...B-7
Perkins...C-7
Perry...B-7
Picher...A-10
Ponca City...B-7
Pryor...B-9
Prague...C-8
Purcell...C-7
Sallisaw...C-10
Sand Springs...B-8
Sapulpa...B-8
Sayre...C-4
Seminole...C-8
Shawnee...B-7
Skiatook...B-8
Spiro...A-10
Stigler...C-9
Stillwater...B-7
Stilwell...C-10
Stroud...C-8
Sulphur...D-7
Tahlequah...C-10
Talihina...C-9
Taloga...B-5
Tecumseh...C-8
Tishomingo...D-7
Tonkawa...B-7
Tulsa...C-7
Vinita...A-9
Wagoner...B-9
Walters...E-6
Weatherford...C-5
Wetumka...C-8
Wewoka...C-8
Wilson...D-7
Woodward...A-7
Wynnewood...C-7

Pg. 28
Pg. 7
Pg. 22
Pg. 47
Pg. 12
Pg. 33
Pg. 46

MO.
ARKANSAS
KANSAS
TEXAS
COLORADO
NEW MEXICO

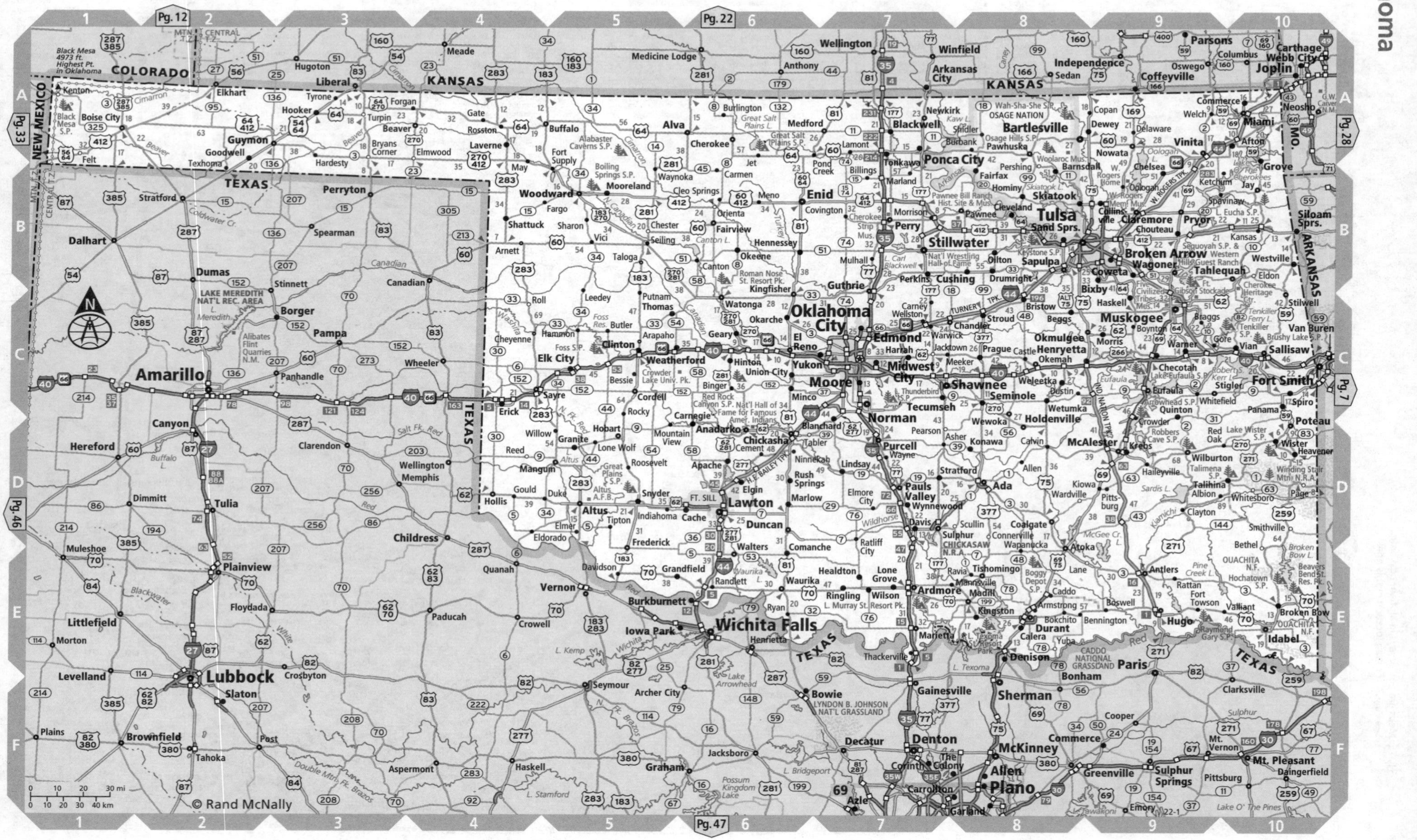

© Rand McNally

NOTE: Maps are not always in alphabetical order.
See Page 1 for map location in this atlas.

Oregon 43

IDAHO

WASHINGTON

NEVADA

CALIFORNIA

PACIFIC OCEAN

© Rand McNally

Oregon

Population: 3,831,074
Land Area: 95,988 sq. mi.
Capital: Salem

Cities and Towns

City	Grid
Albany	C-2
Amity	C-2
Ashland	A-2
Astoria	B-7
Athena	C-8
Baker City	D-8
Bandon	E-1
Beaverton	B-3
Bend	D-4
Boardman	B-6
Brookings	A-1
Bunker Hill	E-1
Burns	D-6
Camas	A-2
Cannon Beach	A-2
Canyon City	D-7
Canyonville	B-2
Central Point	A-2
Clackamas	B-3
Coos Bay	E-1
Coquille	E-1
Corvallis	C-2
Cottage Grove	C-2
Dallas	C-2
Eagle Point	A-2
Enterprise	C-8
Estacada	B-3
Eugene	C-2
Florence	D-1
Fossil	C-5
Gladstone	B-3
Gold Beach	E-1
Grants Pass	A-2
Heppner	C-6
Hermiston	B-7
Hillsboro	B-3
Hood River	A-4
Jacksonville	A-2
John Day	D-7
Junction City	C-2
Klamath Falls	A-3
La Grande	C-8
La Pine	D-4
Lakeside	E-1
Lakeview	A-4
Lebanon	C-2
Madras	C-4
McMinnville	B-3
Medford	A-2
Mill City	C-3
Milton-Freewater	C-8
Molalla	B-3
Monmouth	C-2
Myrtle Creek	B-2
Myrtle Point	E-1
Newberg	B-3
Newport	C-1
North Bend	E-1
Oakridge	C-3
Ontario	D-9
Oregon City	B-3
Pendleton	C-7
Philomath	C-2
Phoenix	A-2
Pilot Rock	C-7
Portland	B-3
Prineville	C-4
Rainier	A-3
Redmond	C-4
Reedsport	D-1
Rockaway Beach	A-2
Roseburg	B-2
St. Helens	A-3
Salem	C-2
Scappoose	A-3
Seaside	A-2
Silverton	C-3
Springfield	C-2
Stayton	C-3
Sublimity	C-3
Sutherlin	B-2
Sweet Home	C-3
The Dalles	A-4
Tigard	B-3
Tillamook	A-2
Toledo	C-1
Umatilla	B-7
Union	C-8
Vale	D-9
Veneta	C-2
Vernonia	A-3
Warm Springs	C-4
Warrenton	A-2
Winston	B-2
Woodburn	C-3

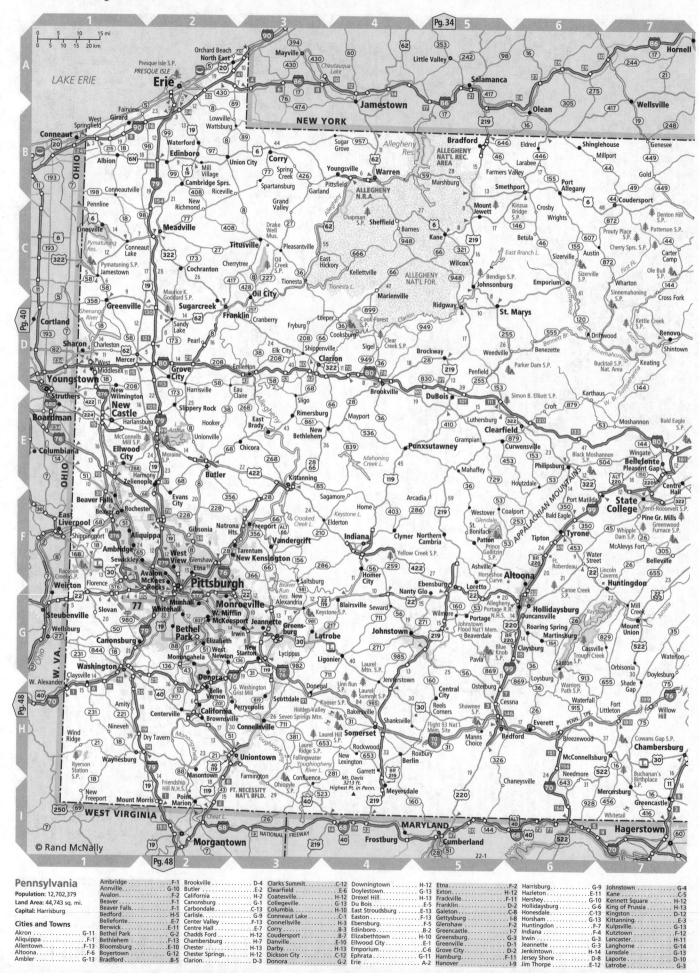

© Rand McNally

Pennsylvania

Population: 12,702,379
Land Area: 44,743 sq. mi.
Capital: Harrisburg

Cities and Towns

Akron G-11	Ambridge F-1	Brookville D-4	Clarks Summit C-12
Aliquippa F-1	Annville G-10	Butler E-2	Clearfield E-6
Allentown F-13	Avalon F-2	California H-2	Coatesville H-12
Altoona F-6	Beaver F-1	Canonsburg G-1	Collegeville G-13
Ambler G-13	Beaver Falls F-1	Carbondale C-13	Columbia H-10
	Bedford H-5	Carlisle G-9	Conneaut Lake C-1
	Bellefonte E-7	Center Valley F-13	Connellsville H-3
	Berwick E-11	Centre Hall E-7	Corry B-3
	Bethel Park G-2	Chadds Ford H-12	Coudersport B-7
	Bethlehem F-13	Chambersburg H-7	Danville E-10
	Bloomsburg E-10	Chester H-13	Darby H-13
	Boyertown G-12	Chester Springs G-12	Dickson City C-12
	Bradford B-5	Clarion D-3	Donora G-2

Downingtown H-12	Etna F-2	Harrisburg G-9
Doylestown G-13	Exton H-12	Hazleton E-11
Drexel Hill H-13	Frackville F-11	Hershey G-10
Du Bois D-5	Franklin D-2	Hollidaysburg G-6
East Stroudsburg E-13	Galeton C-8	Honesdale C-13
Easton F-13	Gettysburg I-8	Horsham G-13
Ebensburg F-4	Glenshaw F-2	Huntingdon F-7
Edinboro B-2	Greencastle I-7	Indiana F-4
Elizabethtown H-10	Greensburg G-3	Irwin G-3
Ellwood City E-1	Grove City D-2	Jeannette G-3
Emporium C-6	Hamburg F-11	Jenkintown H-14
Ephrata G-11	Hanover I-9	Jim Thorpe E-12
Erie A-2		

Johnstown G-4	
Kane C-5	
Kennett Square H-12	
King of Prussia H-13	
Kingston D-12	
Kittanning E-3	
Kulpsville G-13	
Kutztown F-12	
Lancaster H-11	
Langhorne G-14	
Lansdale G-13	
Laporte D-10	
Latrobe G-3	

NOTE: Maps are not always in alphabetical order.
See Page 1 for map location in this atlas.

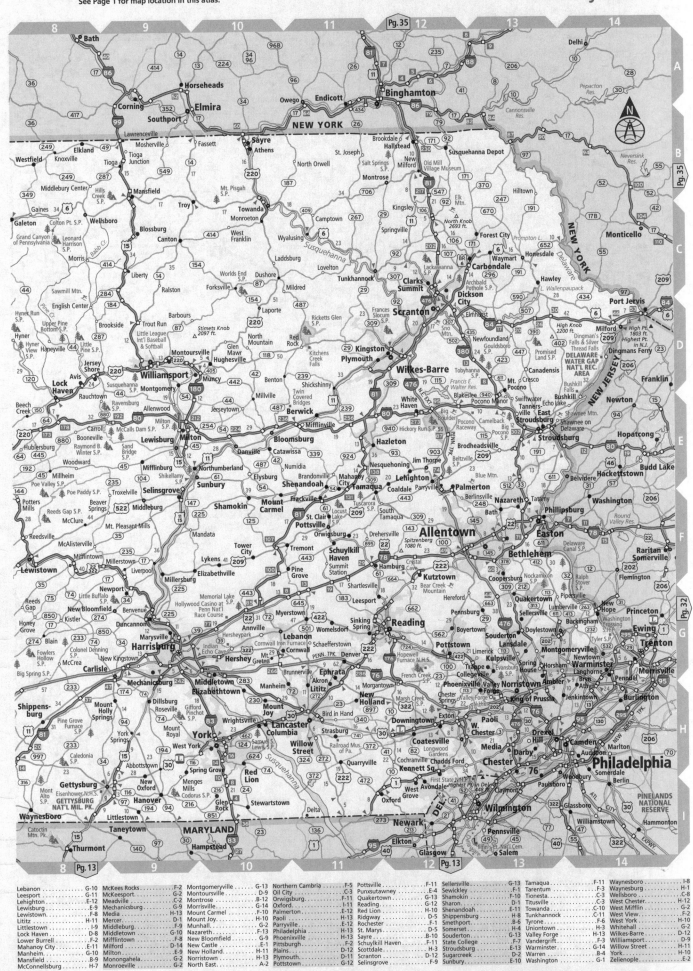

Lebanon	G-10	McKees Rocks	F-2
Leesport	G-11	McKeesport	G-2
Lehighton	E-12	Meadville	C-2
Lewisburg	E-9	Mechanicsburg	G-9
Lewistown	F-8	Media	H-13
Lititz	H-11	Mercer	D-1
Littlestown	I-9	Middleburg	F-9
Lock Haven	D-8	Middletown	G-10
Lower Burrell	F-2	Mifflintown	F-8
Mahanoy City	E-11	Milford	D-14
Manheim	G-10	Milton	E-9
Mansfield	B-8	Monongahela	G-2
McConnellsburg	H-7	Monroeville	G-2

Montgomeryville	G-13	Northern Cambria	F-5
Montoursville	D-9	Oil City	C-3
Montrose	B-12	Orwigsburg	F-11
Morrisville	G-14	Oxford	I-11
Mount Carmel	F-10	Palmerton	E-12
Mount Joy	H-10	Paoli	H-13
Munhall	G-2	Parryville	E-12
Nazareth	F-13	Philadelphia	H-13
New Bloomfield	G-9	Phoenixville	G-13
New Castle	E-1	Pittsburgh	G-2
New Holland	H-11	Plains	D-11
Norristown	H-13	Plymouth	D-11
North East	A-2	Pottstown	G-12

Pottsville	F-11	Sellersville	G-13
Punxsutawney	E-4	Sewickley	F-1
Quakertown	G-13	Shamokin	F-10
Reading	G-12	Sharon	D-1
Red Lion	H-10	Shenandoah	F-11
Ridgway	D-5	Shippensburg	H-8
Rochester	F-1	Smethport	C-5
St. Marys	D-5	Somerset	H-4
Sayre	B-10	Souderton	G-13
Schuylkill Haven	F-11	State College	F-7
Scottdale	H-3	Stroudsburg	E-13
Scranton	D-12	Sugarcreek	D-2
Selinsgrove	F-9	Sunbury	E-10

Tamaqua	F-11	Waynesboro	I-8
Tarentum	F-1	Waynesburg	H-1
Tionesta	C-3	Wellsboro	C-8
Titusville	C-3	West Chester	H-12
Towanda	B-10	West Mifflin	G-2
Tunkhannock	C-11	West View	F-1
Tyrone	F-6	West York	H-10
Uniontown	H-3	Whitehall	G-2
Valley Forge	H-13	Wilkes-Barre	D-12
Vandergrift	F-3	Williamsport	D-9
Warminster	G-14	Willow Street	H-11
Warren	B-4	York	H-10
Washington	G-1	Zelienople	F-1

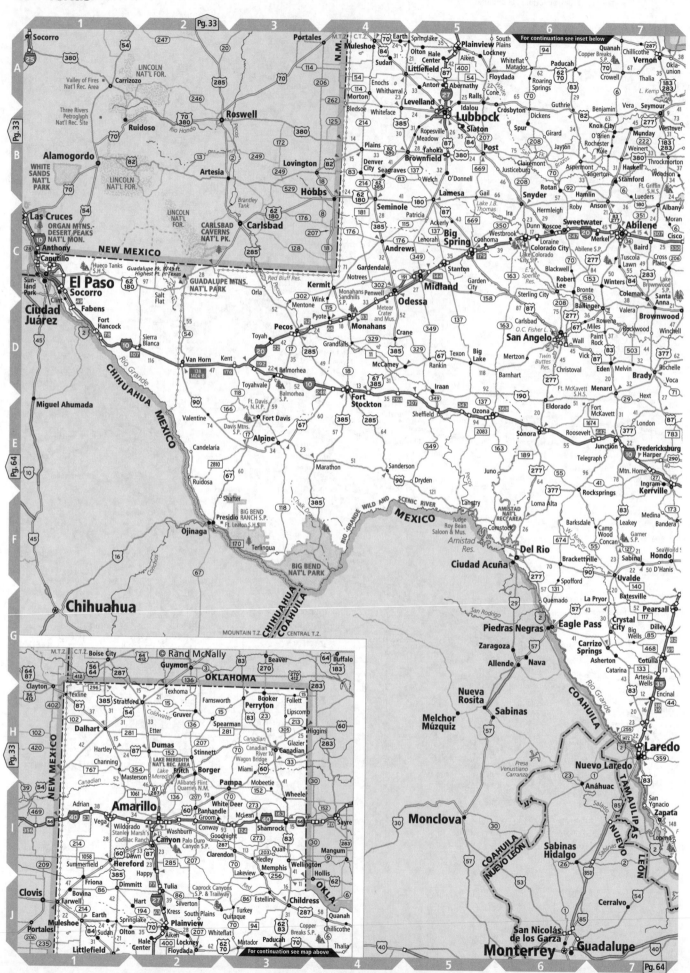

© Rand McNally

For continuation see inset below

For continuation see map above

NOTE: Maps are not always in alphabetical order.
See Page 1 for map location in this atlas.

Texas 47

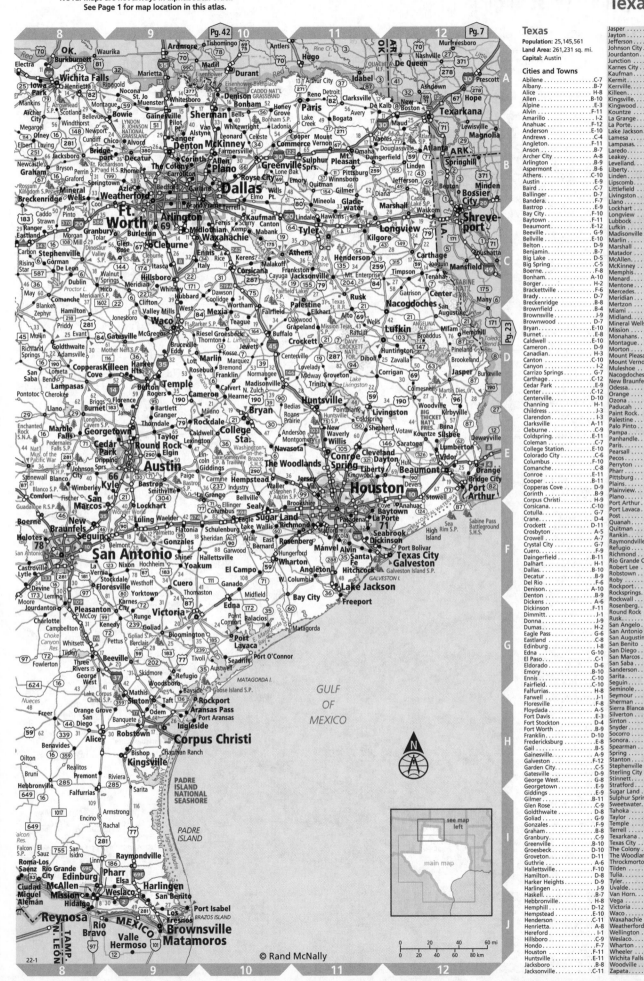

Texas

Population: 25,145,561
Land Area: 261,231 sq. mi.
Capital: Austin

Cities and Towns

Abilene	C-7
Albany	B-7
Alice	H-8
Allen	B-10
Alpine	E-3
Alvin	F-11
Amarillo	I-2
Anahuac	F-12
Anderson	E-10
Andrews	C-4
Angleton	F-11
Anson	B-7
Archer City	A-8
Arlington	B-9
Aspermont	B-6
Athens	C-10
Austin	E-9
Baird	C-7
Ballinger	D-7
Bandera	F-7
Bastrop	E-9
Bay City	F-10
Baytown	F-11
Beaumont	E-12
Beeville	G-9
Bellville	E-10
Belton	D-9
Benjamin	B-7
Big Lake	D-5
Big Spring	C-5
Boerne	F-8
Bonham	A-10
Borger	H-2
Brackettville	F-7
Brady	D-7
Breckenridge	B-8
Brownfield	B-4
Brownsville	J-9
Brownwood	D-7
Bryan	E-10
Burnet	E-8
Caldwell	E-10
Cameron	D-9
Canadian	H-3
Canton	C-9
Canyon	I-2
Carrizo Springs	G-7
Carthage	C-12
Cedar Park	E-9
Center	C-12
Centerville	D-10
Channing	H-1
Childress	J-3
Clarendon	I-3
Clarksville	A-11
Cleburne	C-9
Coldspring	E-11
Coleman	C-7
College Station	E-10
Colorado City	C-6
Columbus	F-10
Comanche	C-8
Conroe	E-11
Cooper	B-11
Copperas Cove	D-9
Corinth	B-9
Corpus Christi	H-9
Corsicana	C-10
Cotulla	G-7
Crane	D-4
Crockett	D-11
Crosbyton	A-5
Crowell	A-7
Crystal City	G-7
Cuero	F-9
Daingerfield	B-11
Dalhart	H-1
Dallas	B-9
Decatur	B-9
Del Rio	F-6
Denison	A-10
Denton	B-9
Dickens	A-6
Dickinson	F-11
Dimmitt	J-1
Donna	J-9
Dumas	H-2
Eagle Pass	G-6
Eastland	C-8
Edinburg	I-8
Edna	G-10
El Paso	C-1
Eldorado	D-6
Emory	B-10
Ennis	C-10
Fairfield	C-10
Falfurrias	H-8
Farwell	J-1
Floresville	F-8
Floydada	A-5
Fort Davis	D-3
Fort Stockton	D-4
Fort Worth	B-9
Franklin	D-10
Fredericksburg	E-8
Gail	B-5
Gainesville	A-9
Galveston	F-12
Garden City	C-5
Gatesville	D-9
George West	G-8
Georgetown	E-9
Giddings	E-9
Gilmer	B-11
Glen Rose	C-9
Goldthwaite	D-8
Goliad	G-9
Gonzales	F-9
Graham	B-8
Granbury	C-9
Greenville	B-10
Groesbeck	D-10
Groveton	D-11
Guthrie	A-6
Hallettsville	F-10
Hamilton	D-8
Harker Heights	D-9
Harlingen	J-9
Haskell	B-7
Hebbronville	H-8
Hemphill	D-12
Hempstead	E-10
Henderson	C-11
Henrietta	A-8
Hereford	I-1
Hillsboro	C-9
Hondo	F-7
Houston	F-11
Huntsville	E-11
Jacksboro	B-8
Jacksonville	C-11

Jasper	D-12
Jayton	B-6
Jefferson	B-12
Johnson City	E-8
Jourdanton	G-8
Junction	E-7
Karnes City	G-9
Kaufman	C-10
Kermit	C-4
Kerrville	E-7
Killeen	D-9
Kingsville	H-9
Kingwood	E-11
Kountze	E-12
La Grange	E-10
La Porte	F-11
Lake Jackson	F-11
Lamesa	B-5
Lampasas	D-8
Laredo	H-7
Leakey	F-7
Levelland	A-4
Liberty	E-11
Linden	B-12
Lipscomb	H-3
Littlefield	A-4
Livingston	E-11
Llano	E-8
Lockhart	F-9
Longview	C-11
Lubbock	B-5
Lufkin	D-12
Madisonville	D-10
Marlin	D-9
Marshall	C-12
Matador	A-6
McAllen	J-8
McKinney	B-10
Memphis	I-3
Menard	D-7
Mentone	C-3
Mercedes	J-9
Meridian	C-9
Mertzon	D-6
Miami	H-3
Midland	C-5
Mineral Wells	B-8
Mission	I-8
Monahans	D-4
Montague	A-9
Morton	A-4
Mount Pleasant	B-11
Mount Vernon	B-11
Muleshoe	J-1
Nacogdoches	D-12
New Braunfels	F-8
Odessa	C-4
Orange	E-12
Ozona	E-5
Paducah	A-6
Paint Rock	D-7
Palestine	C-11
Palo Pinto	B-8
Pampa	I-3
Panhandle	I-2
Paris	A-11
Pearsall	G-7
Pecos	D-3
Perryton	H-3
Pharr	J-8
Pittsburg	B-11
Plains	B-4
Plainview	J-2
Plano	B-10
Port Arthur	E-12
Port Lavaca	G-10
Post	B-5
Quanah	J-4
Quitman	B-11
Rankin	D-5
Raymondville	I-9
Refugio	G-9
Richmond	F-11
Rio Grande City	I-8
Robert Lee	C-6
Robstown	H-9
Roby	B-6
Rockport	H-9
Rocksprings	E-6
Rockwall	B-10
Rosenberg	F-11
Round Rock	E-9
Rusk	C-11
San Angelo	D-6
San Antonio	F-8
San Augustine	D-12
San Benito	J-9
San Diego	H-8
San Marcos	F-9
San Saba	D-8
Sanderson	E-4
Sarita	H-9
Seguin	F-9
Seminole	B-4
Seymour	A-7
Sherman	A-10
Sierra Blanca	D-2
Silverton	J-2
Sinton	H-9
Snyder	B-6
Socorro	C-1
Sonora	E-6
Spearman	H-2
Spring	E-11
Stanton	C-5
Stephenville	C-8
Sterling City	C-6
Stinnett	H-2
Stratford	H-2
Sugar Land	F-11
Sulphur Springs	B-11
Sweetwater	C-6
Tahoka	B-5
Taylor	E-9
Temple	D-9
Terrell	B-10
Texarkana	B-12
Texas City	F-11
The Colony	B-9
The Woodlands	E-11
Throckmorton	B-7
Tilden	G-8
Tulia	J-2
Tyler	C-11
Uvalde	F-7
Van Horn	D-2
Vega	I-1
Victoria	G-9
Waco	D-9
Waxahachie	C-9
Weatherford	B-9
Wellington	I-3
Weslaco	J-9
Wharton	F-10
Wheeler	I-3
Wichita Falls	A-8
Woodville	D-12
Zapata	I-7

© Rand McNally

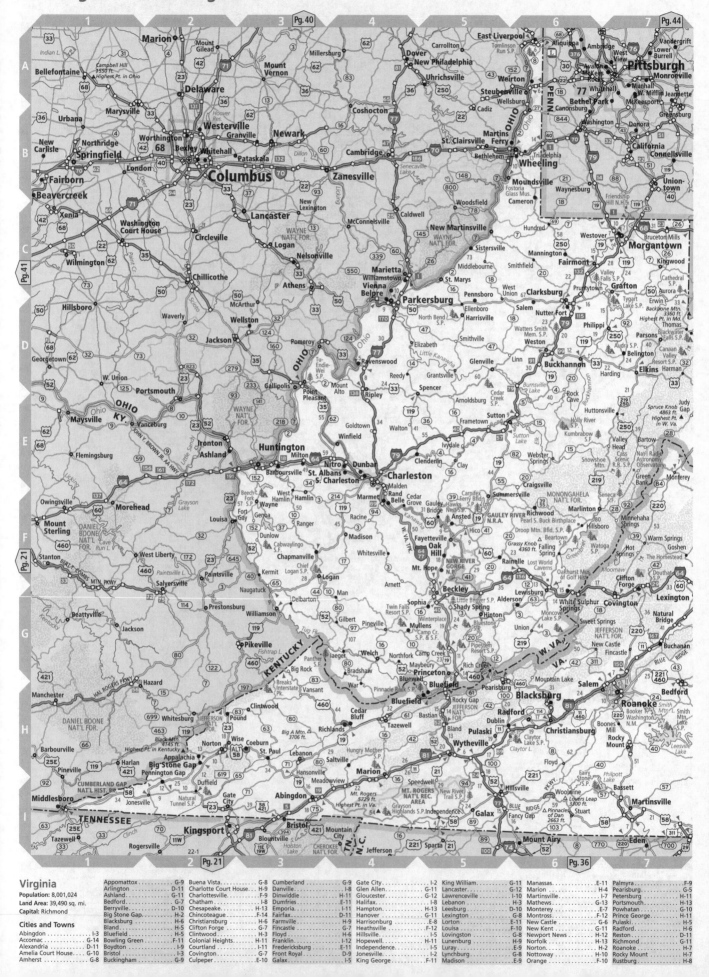

Virginia

Population: 8,001,024
Land Area: 39,490 sq. mi.
Capital: Richmond

Cities and Towns

Abingdon	I-3
Accomac	G-14
Alexandria	D-11
Amelia Court House	G-10
Amherst	G-8
Appomattox	G-9
Arlington	D-11
Ashland	G-11
Bedford	G-7
Berryville	D-10
Big Stone Gap	I-2
Blacksburg	H-6
Bland	H-5
Bluefield	H-5
Bowling Green	F-11
Boydton	I-9
Bristol	I-3
Buckingham	G-9
Buena Vista	G-8
Charlotte Court House	H-9
Charlottesville	F-9
Chatham	H-8
Chesapeake	H-13
Chincoteague	F-14
Christiansburg	H-6
Clifton Forge	G-7
Clintwood	H-3
Colonial Heights	G-10
Courtland	I-11
Covington	G-7
Culpeper	E-10
Cumberland	G-9
Danville	I-8
Dinwiddie	H-10
Dumfries	E-11
Emporia	I-11
Fairfax	D-11
Fincastle	G-7
Floyd	H-6
Franklin	I-11
Fredericksburg	E-11
Front Royal	D-9
Galax	I-5
Gate City	I-2
Glen Allen	G-11
Gloucester	G-12
Halifax	I-8
Hampton	H-12
Hanover	G-11
Harrisonburg	E-8
Heathsville	F-12
Hillsville	I-5
Hopewell	H-11
Independence	I-5
Jonesville	I-2
King George	F-11
King William	G-11
Lancaster	G-12
Lawrenceville	I-10
Lebanon	H-3
Leesburg	D-10
Lexington	G-8
Lorton	E-11
Louisa	F-10
Lovingston	G-8
Lunenburg	H-9
Luray	E-9
Lynchburg	G-8
Madison	E-9
Manassas	E-11
Marion	H-4
Martinsville	I-7
Mathews	G-13
Monterey	E-7
Montross	F-12
New Castle	G-6
New Kent	G-11
Newport News	H-12
Norfolk	H-13
Norton	H-2
Nottoway	H-10
Orange	E-9
Palmyra	F-9
Pearisburg	G-5
Petersburg	H-11
Portsmouth	H-13
Powhatan	G-10
Prince George	H-11
Pulaski	H-5
Radford	H-6
Reston	D-11
Richmond	G-11
Roanoke	H-7
Rocky Mount	H-7
Rustburg	H-8

NOTE: Maps are not always in alphabetical order.
See Page 1 for map location in this atlas.

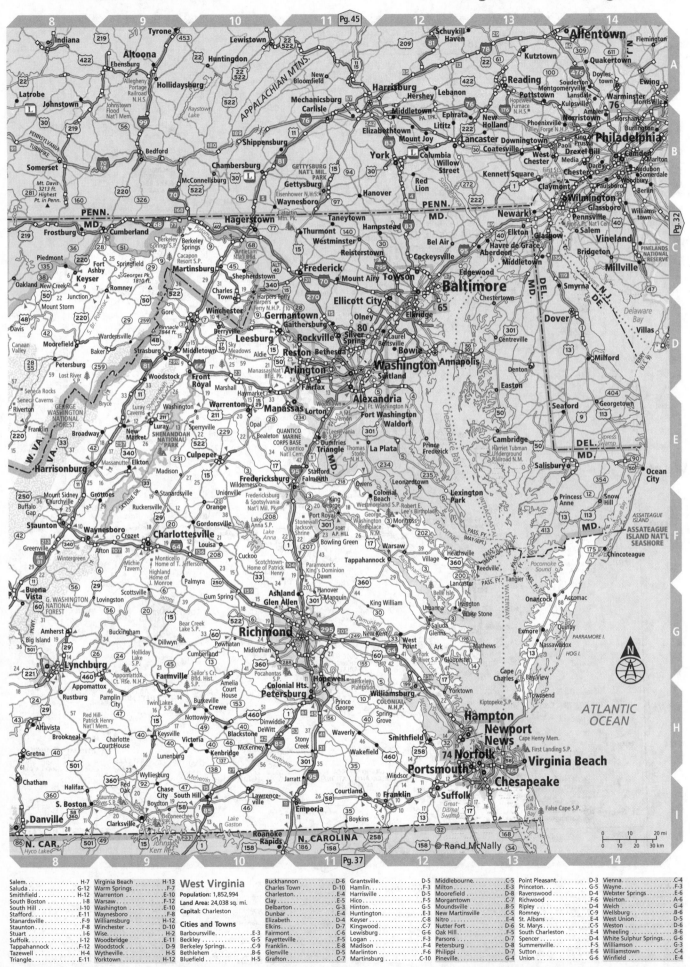

Salem. H-7	Virginia Beach. H-13	**West Virginia**	Buckhannon. D-6	Grantsville. D-5
Saluda. G-12	Warm Springs. F-7	Population: 1,852,994	Charles Town. D-10	Hamlin. E-3
Smithfield. H-12	Warrenton. E-10	Land Area: 24,038 sq. mi.	Charleston. E-4	Harrisville. D-5
South Boston. I-8	Warsaw. F-12	Capital: Charleston	Clay. E-5	Hico. F-5
South Hill. I-10	Washington. E-10		Delbarton. G-3	Hinton. F-5
Stafford. E-11	Waynesboro. F-8	**Cities and Towns**	Dunbar. E-4	Huntington. E-3
Stanardsville. F-9	Williamsburg. H-12	Barboursville. E-3	Elizabeth. D-4	Keyser. C-8
Staunton. F-8	Winchester. D-10	Beckley. G-5	Elkins. E-7	Kingwood. C-7
Stuart. I-6	Wise. H-2	Berkeley Springs. C-9	Fairmont. C-6	Lewisburg. G-6
Suffolk. I-12	Woodbridge. E-11	Bethlehem. B-6	Fayetteville. F-5	Logan. G-4
Tappahannock. F-12	Woodstock. D-9	Bluefield. H-5	Franklin. E-8	Madison. F-4
Tazewell. H-4	Wytheville. H-4		Glenville. D-5	Marlinton. F-7
Triangle. E-11	Yorktown. H-12		Grafton. C-7	Martinsburg. C-10

Middlebourne. C-5	Point Pleasant. D-3	Vienna. C-4
Milton. E-3	Princeton. G-5	Wayne. F-3
Moorefield. D-8	Ravenswood. D-4	Webster Springs. E-6
Morgantown. B-6	Richwood. F-6	Weirton. A-6
Moundsville. B-5	Ripley. D-4	Welch. G-4
New Martinsville. C-5	Romney. C-9	Wellsburg. B-6
Nitro. E-4	St. Albans. E-4	West Union. D-5
Nutter Fort. D-6	St. Marys. C-5	Weston. D-6
Oak Hill. F-5	South Charleston. E-4	Wheeling. B-6
Parsons. D-7	Spencer. D-4	White Sulphur Springs. .G-6
Petersburg. D-8	Summersville. E-6	Williamson. G-3
Philippi. C-7	Sutton. E-6	Williamstown. C-4
Pineville. G-4	Union. G-6	Winfield. E-4

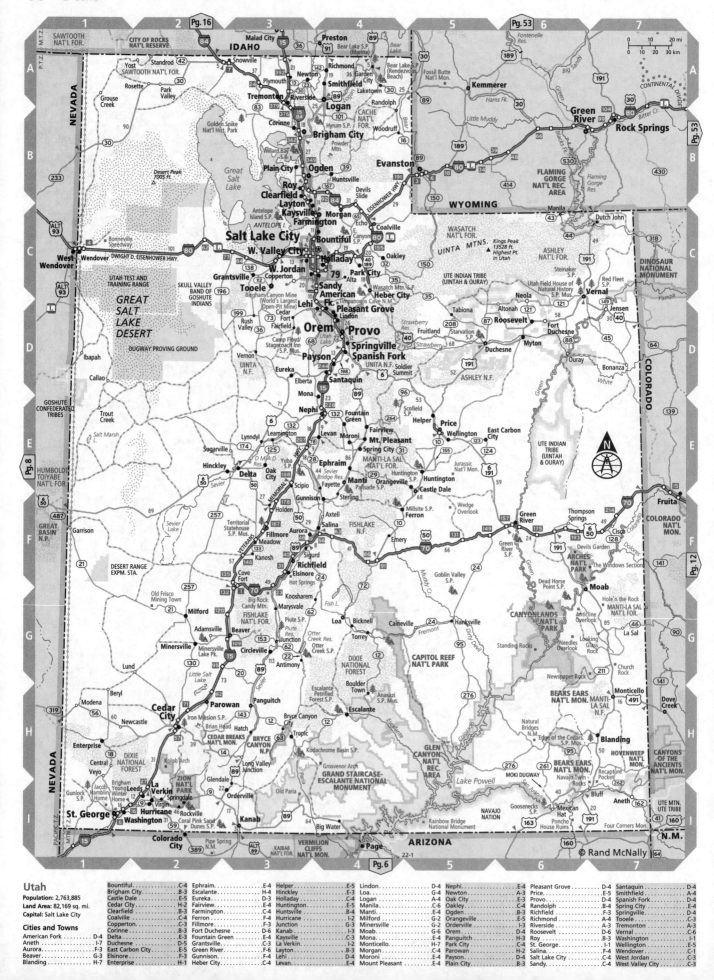

Utah

Population: 2,763,885
Land Area: 82,169 sq. mi.
Capital: Salt Lake City

Cities and Towns

American Fork	D-4
Aneth	I-7
Aurora	F-3
Beaver	G-3
Blanding	H-7
Bountiful	C-4
Brigham City	B-3
Castle Dale	E-5
Cedar City	H-2
Clearfield	B-3
Coalville	C-4
Corinne	B-3
Delta	E-3
Duchesne	D-5
East Carbon City	E-5
Elsinore	F-3
Enterprise	H-1
Ephraim	E-4
Escalante	H-4
Eureka	D-3
Fairview	E-4
Farmington	C-4
Ferron	F-4
Fillmore	E-3
Fort Duchesne	D-6
Fountain Green	E-4
Grantsville	C-3
Green River	F-6
Gunnison	F-4
Heber City	C-4
Helper	E-5
Hinckley	E-3
Holladay	C-4
Huntington	E-5
Huntsville	B-4
Hurricane	I-2
Junction	G-3
Kanab	I-3
Kaysville	C-4
La Verkin	I-2
Layton	B-3
Lehi	D-4
Levan	E-4
Lindon	D-4
Loa	G-4
Logan	A-4
Manila	C-6
Manti	E-4
Milford	G-2
Minersville	G-2
Moab	G-6
Mona	E-4
Monticello	H-7
Morgan	C-4
Moroni	E-4
Mount Pleasant	E-4
Nephi	E-4
Newton	A-3
Oak City	E-3
Oakley	C-4
Ogden	B-3
Orangeville	E-5
Orderville	I-3
Orem	D-4
Panguitch	H-3
Park City	C-4
Parowan	H-2
Payson	D-4
Plain City	B-3
Pleasant Grove	D-4
Price	E-5
Provo	D-4
Randolph	B-4
Richfield	F-3
Richmond	A-4
Riverside	A-3
Roosevelt	D-6
Roy	B-3
St. George	I-1
Salina	F-4
Salt Lake City	C-4
Sandy	C-4
Santaquin	D-4
Smithfield	A-4
Spanish Fork	D-4
Spring City	E-4
Springville	D-4
Tooele	C-3
Tremonton	A-3
Vernal	C-6
Washington	I-1
Wellington	E-5
Wendover	C-1
West Jordan	C-3
West Valley City	C-4

NOTE: Maps are not always in alphabetical order.
See Page 1 for map location in this atlas.

Washington **51**

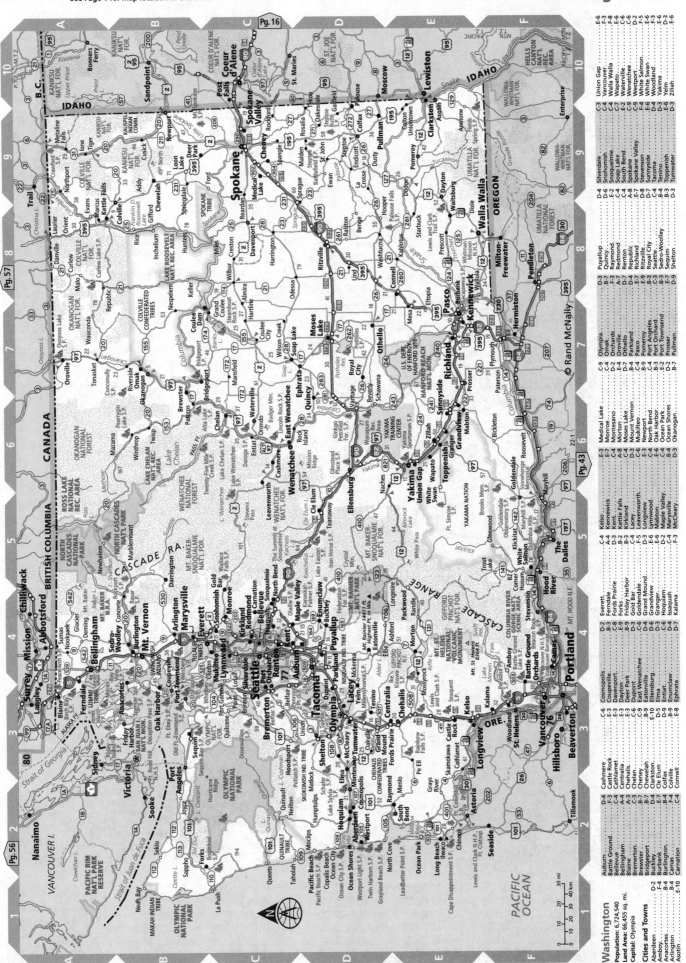

Washington

Population: 6,724,540
Land Area: 66,455 sq. mi.
Capital: Olympia

Cities and Towns

Aberdeen	D-2
Amboy	B-4
Anacortes	B-4
Arlington	B-4
Asotin	E-10

Auburn	D-4
Battle Ground	C-4
Bellevue	D-4
Bellingham	A-4
Blaine	A-3
Bremerton	C-3
Brewster	B-7
Bridgeport	B-7
Buckley	D-4
Burlington	B-4
Camas	C-4
Carnation	C-4

Cashmere	D-4
Castle Rock	C-4
Cathlamet	C-4
Centralia	C-3
Chehalis	C-3
Chelan	C-6
Cheney	B-9
Chewelah	A-9
Clarkston	E-10
Colfax	E-10
Colville	A-9
Connell	C-8

Cosmopolis	C-6
Coupeville	B-3
Davenport	B-9
Dayton	E-3
Deer Park	C-6
Dupont	C-3
East Wenatchee	C-6
Eatonville	D-6
Edmonds	D-6
Ellensburg	D-5
Elma	D-5
Entiat	D-9
Enumclaw	D-7
Ephrata	C-8

Everett	D-2
Ferndale	B-3
Fords Prairie	F-3
Forks	B-9
Friday Harbor	B-4
Gold Bar	C-6
Goldendale	C-4
Granger	D-6
Grandview	D-6
Grand Mound	C-4
Hoquiam	C-4
Issaquah	D-2
Kalama	D-7

Kelso	C-4
Kennewick	A-4
Kent	B-2
Kettle Falls	C-4
Kirkland	C-4
Lacey	E-6
Leavenworth	E-3
Longview	E-6
Mabton	B-3
Maple Valley	D-6
Marysville	D-2
McCleary	F-3

Medical Lake	C-9
Monroe	E-7
Montesano	D-2
Morton	A-8
Moses Lake	D-7
Mount Vernon	A-8
Mukilteo	C-4
Newport	E-7
North Bend	E-3
Oak Harbor	E-6
Ocean Park	D-2
Ocean Shores	B-4
Okanogan	D-3

Olympia	C-9
Omak	A-4
Orchards	D-2
Oroville	D-7
Othello	B-6
Pasco	D-7
Pomeroy	E-9
Port Angeles	B-3
Port Orchard	C-4
Port Townsend	D-2
Prosser	B-7
Pullman	D-9

Puyallup	D-3
Quincy	B-7
Raymond	F-3
Redmond	C-4
Renton	E-2
Republic	D-7
Richland	D-7
Ritzville	A-8
Royal City	B-3
Seattle	C-4
Sedro-Woolley	B-3
Sequim	E-7
Shelton	D-3

Silverdale	D-4
Snohomish	D-6
Snoqualmie	F-3
Soap Lake	C-4
Spokane	E-2
Spokane Valley	D-4
Stevenson	F-4
Sunnyside	E-6
Sunnyside	D-7
Tacoma	C-4
Tenino	B-3
Toppenish	E-7
Tumwater	D-3

Union Gap	E-6
Vancouver	C-3
Walla Walla	F-3
Waterville	E-6
Wenatchee	C-6
Westport	D-2
White Salmon	F-5
White Swan	E-6
Woodland	A-6
Yakima	D-3
Zillah	D-3

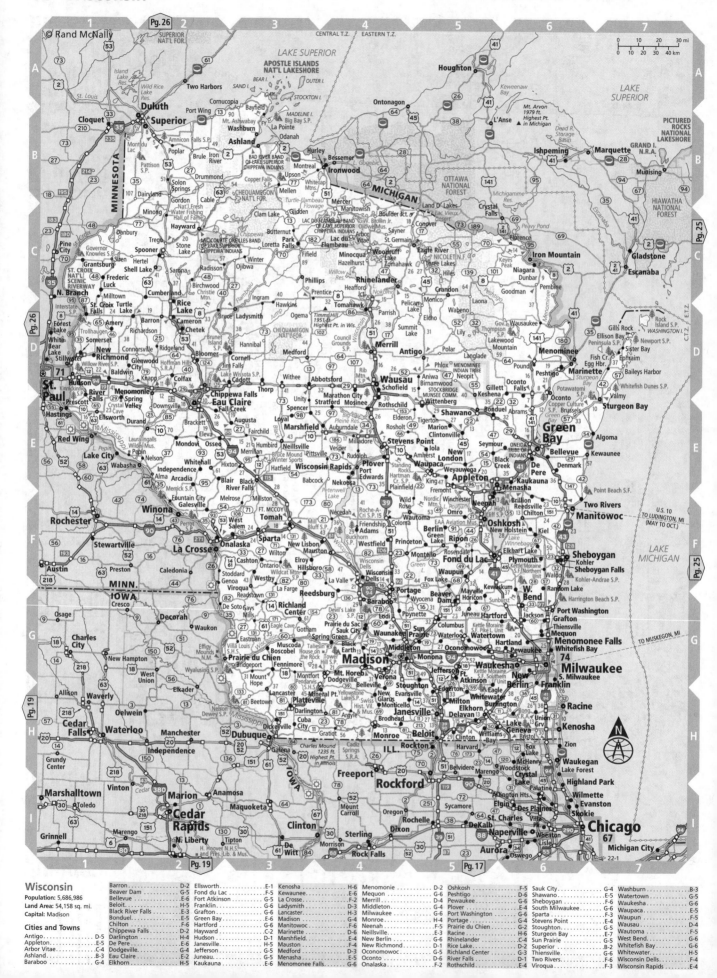

© Rand McNally

Wisconsin

Population: 5,686,986
Land Area: 54,158 sq. mi.
Capital: Madison

Cities and Towns

Antigo	D-5	Barron	D-2	Ellsworth	E-1
Appleton	E-5	Beaver Dam	G-5	Fond du Lac	F-5
Arbor Vitae	C-4	Bellevue	E-6	Fort Atkinson	G-5
Ashland	B-3	Beloit	H-5	Franklin	G-6
Baraboo	G-4	Black River Falls	E-3	Grafton	G-6
		Bonduel	E-5	Green Bay	E-6
		Chilton	F-6	Hartford	G-5
		Chippewa Falls	D-2	Hayward	C-2
		Darlington	H-4	Hudson	D-1
		Dodgeville	G-4	Janesville	H-5
		Eau Claire	E-2	Jefferson	G-5
		Elkhorn	H-5	Juneau	G-5
				Kaukauna	E-6

Kenosha	H-6	Menomonie	D-2	Oshkosh	F-5
Kewaunee	E-6	Mequon	G-6	Peshtigo	D-6
La Crosse	F-2	Merrill	D-4	Pewaukee	G-6
Ladysmith	D-3	Middleton	G-4	Plover	E-4
Lancaster	H-3	Milwaukee	G-6	Port Washington	G-6
Madison	G-4	Monroe	H-4	Portage	G-4
Manitowoc	F-6	Neenah	F-5	Prairie du Chien	G-2
Marinette	D-6	Neillsville	E-3	Racine	H-6
Marshfield	E-4	New Berlin	G-6	Rhinelander	C-4
Mauston	F-4	New Richmond	D-1	Rice Lake	D-2
Medford	D-3	Oconomowoc	G-5	Richland Center	G-3
Menasha	E-5	Oconto	D-6	River Falls	D-1
Menomonee Falls	G-6	Onalaska	F-2	Rothschild	E-4

Sauk City	G-4	Washburn	B-3
Shawano	G-4	Watertown	G-5
Sheboygan	F-6	Waukesha	G-6
South Milwaukee	G-6	Waupaca	E-5
Sparta	F-3	Waupun	F-5
Stevens Point	E-4	Wausau	D-4
Stoughton	G-5	Wautoma	F-4
Sturgeon Bay	E-7	West Bend	G-6
Sun Prairie	G-5	Whitefish Bay	G-6
Superior	B-2	Whitewater	H-5
Thiensville	G-6	Wisconsin Dells	F-4
Two Rivers	F-6	Wisconsin Rapids	E-4
Viroqua	G-3	

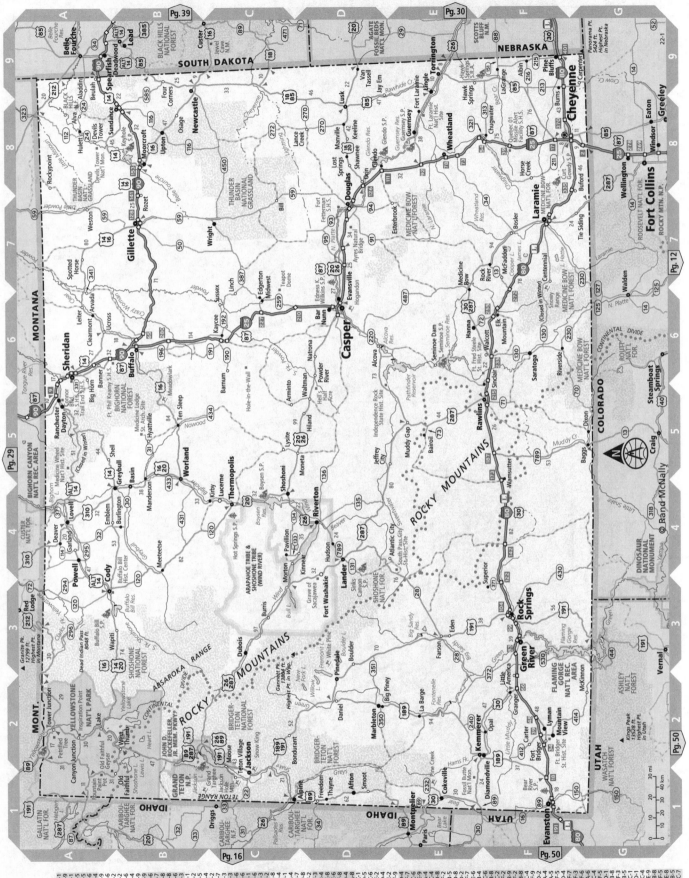

Wyoming

Population: 563,626
Land Area: 97,093 sq. mi.
Capital: Cheyenne

Cities and Towns
Afton D-1
Albin F-9
Alpine C-1
Baggs E-5
Bar Nunn D-6
Basin B-4
Beulah A-9
Big Horn B-5
Big Piney D-2
Bondurant C-2
Buffalo B-6
Burlington B-4
Burns F-9
Carpenter G-9
Casper D-6
Centennial F-7
Chugwater E-8
Clearmont B-6
Cody B-3
Cokeville D-1
Daniel C-2
Dayton B-5
Deaver A-4
Diamondville D-1
Douglas D-7
Dubois C-3
Eden D-3
Edgerton C-6
Elk Mountain E-6
Emblem B-4
Evanston F-1
Evansville D-6
Farson D-3
Fort Bridger E-2
Fort Laramie E-9
Fort Washakie C-4
Freedom C-1
Garland A-4
Gillette B-7
Glendo D-8
Glenrock D-7
Granger E-2
Greybull B-4
Guernsey D-8
Hanna E-6
Horse Creek E-8
Hudson C-4
Hulett A-8
Jackson C-1
Jeffrey City D-5
Kaycee C-6
Keeline D-8
Kemmerer D-1
Kinnear C-4
LaGrange F-9
La Barge D-2
Lander D-4
Laramie E-7
Lingle E-9
Lovell A-4
Lusk D-8
Lyman E-2
Manderson B-4
Manville D-8
McFadden E-7
Medicine Bow E-6
Meeteetse B-4
Midwest C-6
Moorcroft B-8
Mountain View E-2
Newcastle B-8
Opal D-2
Pavillion C-4
Pine Bluffs F-9
Pinedale C-2
Powell A-4
Ranchester B-5
Rawlins E-6
Riverton C-4
Rock River E-7
Rock Springs D-3
Saratoga E-6
Sheridan B-5
Shoshoni C-4
Sinclair E-6
Smoot D-1
Sundance B-8
Ten Sleep B-5
Teton Village C-1
Thayne C-1
Thermopolis C-4
Torrington E-9
Upton B-8
Wamsutter E-5
Wheatland E-8
Worland B-4
Wright C-7

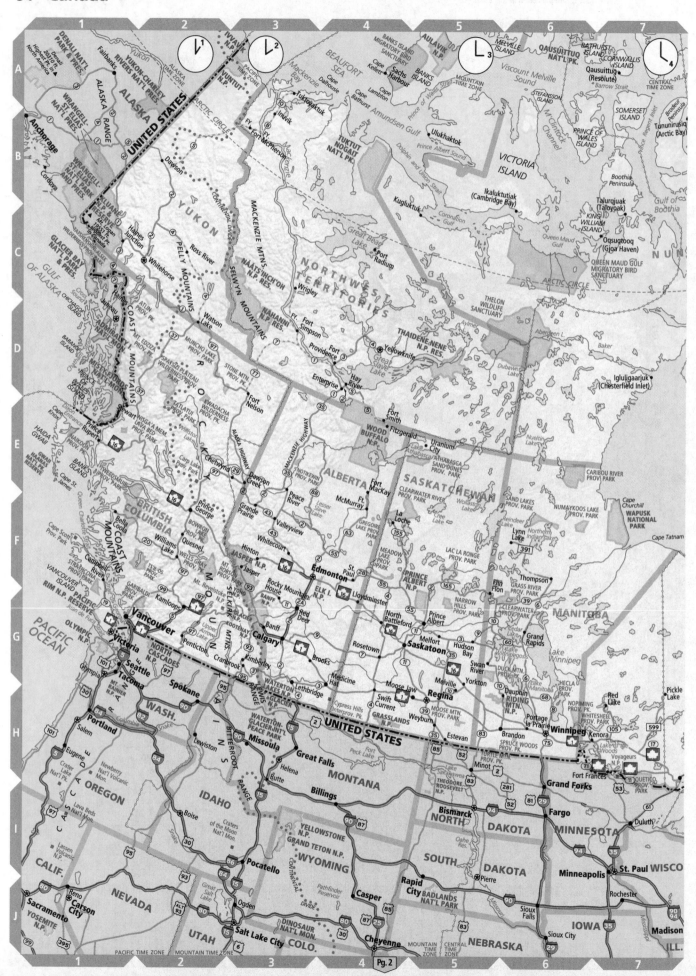

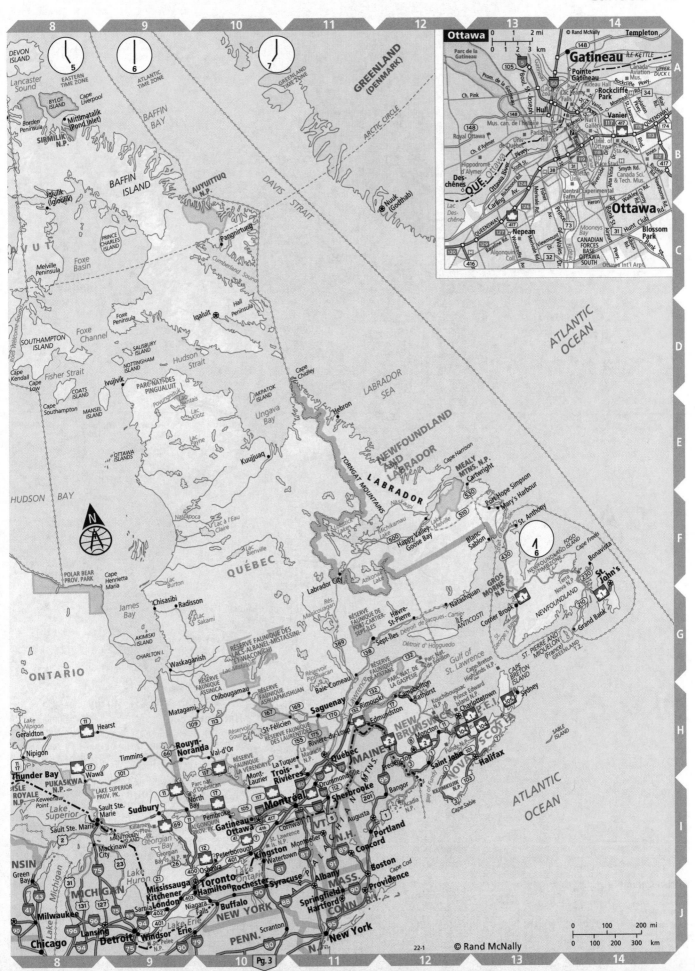

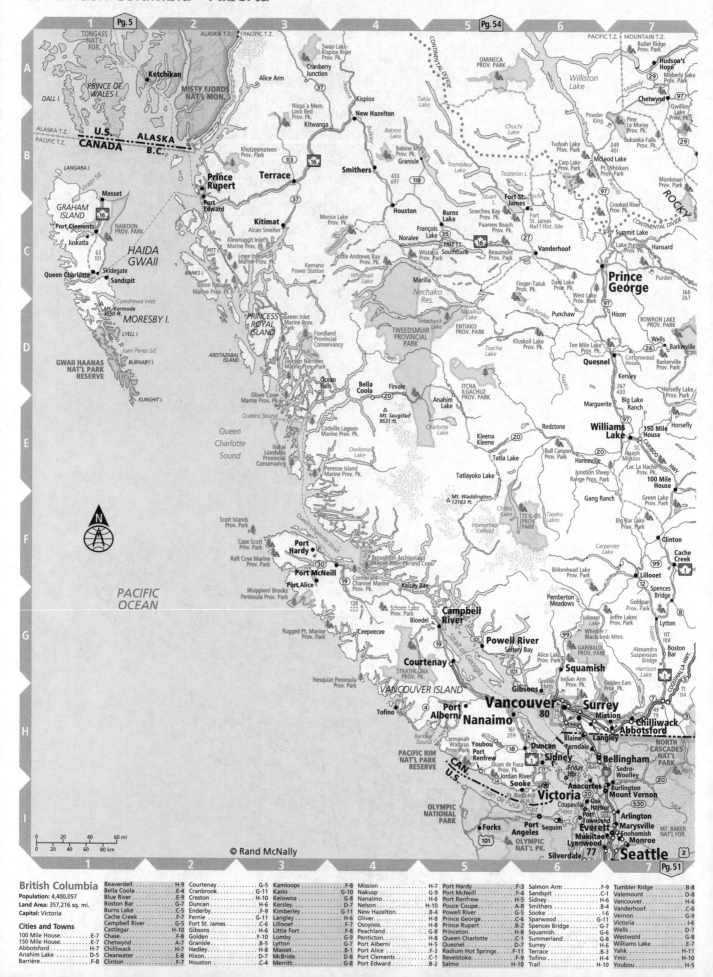

British Columbia

Population: 4,400,057
Land Area: 357,216 sq. mi.
Capital: Victoria

Cities and Towns

100 Mile House	E-7	
150 Mile House	E-7	
Abbotsford	H-7	
Anahim Lake	D-5	
Barrière	F-8	

Beaverdell	H-9
Bella Coola	E-4
Blue River	E-9
Boston Bar	G-7
Burns Lake	C-5
Cache Creek	F-7
Campbell River	G-5
Castlegar	H-10
Chase	F-8
Chetwynd	A-7
Chilliwack	H-7
Clearwater	E-8
Clinton	F-7

Courtenay	G-5
Cranbrook	G-11
Creston	H-10
Duncan	H-6
Enderby	F-9
Fernie	G-11
Fort St. James	B-5
Gibsons	H-6
Golden	F-10
Granisle	B-5
Hedley	H-8
Hixon	D-7
Houston	C-4

Kamloops	F-8
Kaslo	G-10
Kelowna	G-8
Kersley	D-7
Kimberley	G-11
Langley	H-6
Lillooet	F-7
Little Fort	F-8
Lumby	G-9
Lytton	G-7
Masset	B-1
McBride	D-8
Merritt	G-8

Mission	H-7
Nakusp	G-9
Nanaimo	H-6
Nelson	H-10
New Hazelton	B-4
Oliver	H-8
Osoyoos	H-8
Peachland	G-8
Penticton	H-8
Port Alberni	H-5
Port Alice	F-3
Port Clements	C-1
Port Edward	B-2

Port Hardy	F-3
Port McNeill	F-4
Port Renfrew	H-5
Pouce Coupe	A-8
Powell River	G-5
Prince George	C-6
Prince Rupert	B-2
Princeton	H-8
Quesnel	D-7
Radium Hot Springs	F-11
Revelstoke	F-9
Salmo	H-10

Salmon Arm	F-9
Sandspit	C-1
Sidney	H-6
Smithers	B-4
Sooke	I-6
Sparwood	G-11
Spences Bridge	G-7
Squamish	G-6
Summerland	G-8
Surrey	H-6
Terrace	B-3
Tofino	H-4
Trail	H-10

Tumbler Ridge	B-8
Valemount	D-8
Vancouver	H-6
Vanderhoof	C-6
Vernon	G-9
Victoria	I-6
Wells	D-7
Westwold	G-8
Williams Lake	E-7
Yahk	H-11
Ymir	H-10
Youbou	H-6

NOTE: Maps are not always in alphabetical order.
See Page 1 for map location in this atlas.

British Columbia • Alberta 57

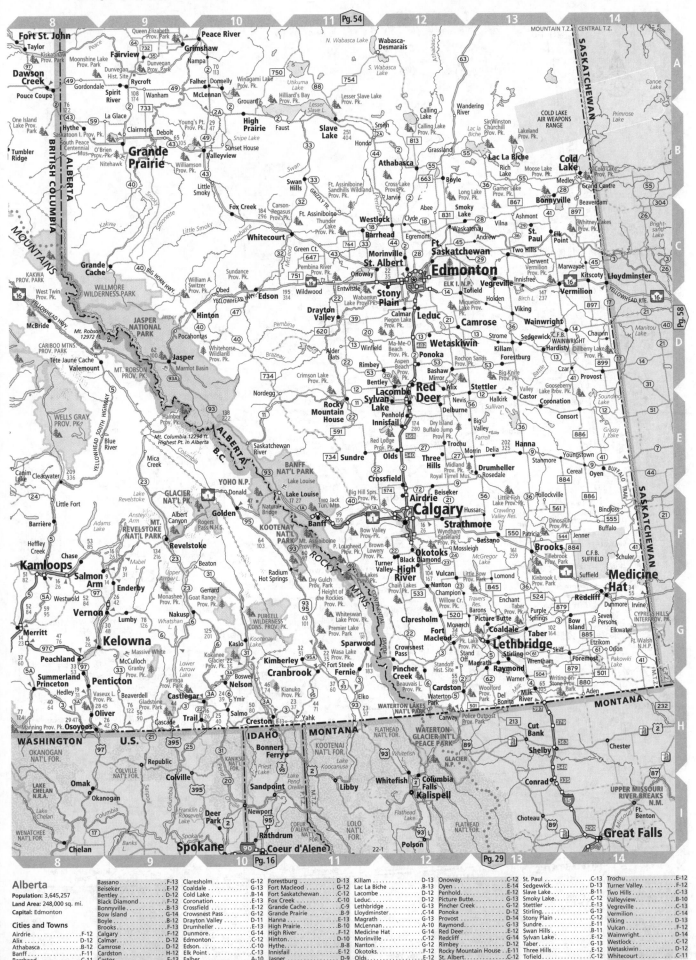

Alberta

Population: 3,645,257
Land Area: 248,000 sq. mi.
Capital: Edmonton

Cities and Towns

Airdrie F-12
Alix D-12
Athabasca B-12
Banff F-11
Barrhead C-11

Bassano F-13
Beiseker F-12
Bentley D-12
Black Diamond F-12
Bonnyville B-13
Bow Island G-14
Boyle B-12
Brooks F-13
Calgary F-12
Calmar D-12
Camrose D-12
Cardston H-12
Castor E-13

Claresholm G-12
Coaldale G-13
Cold Lake B-14
Coronation E-13
Crossfield F-12
Crowsnest Pass G-12
Drayton Valley D-11
Drumheller E-13
Dunmore G-14
Edmonton C-12
Edson C-10
Elk Point C-13
Falher A-10

Forestburg D-13
Fort Macleod G-12
Fort Saskatchewan . . C-12
Fox Creek C-10
Grande Cache C-9
Grande Prairie B-9
Hanna E-13
High Prairie B-10
High River F-12
Hinton C-10
Hythe B-8
Innisfail E-12
Jasper D-9

Killam D-13
Lac La Biche B-13
Lacombe D-12
Leduc D-12
Lethbridge G-13
Lloydminster C-14
Magrath G-13
McLennan A-10
Medicine Hat G-14
Morinville C-12
Nanton G-12
Okotoks F-12
Olds E-12

Onoway C-12
Oyen E-14
Penhold E-12
Picture Butte G-13
Ponoka D-12
Provost D-14
Red Deer E-12
Redcliff G-14
Rimbey D-12
Rocky Mountain House E-11
St. Albert C-12

St. Paul C-13
Sedgewick D-13
Slave Lake B-11
Smoky Lake C-13
Stettler E-13
Stirling G-13
Stony Plain C-12
Sundre E-11
Swan Hills B-11
Sylvan Lake D-12
Taber G-13
Three Hills E-12
Tofield C-12

Trochu E-12
Turner Valley F-12
Two Hills C-13
Valleyview B-10
Vegreville C-13
Vermilion C-14
Viking D-13
Vulcan F-12
Wainwright D-14
Westlock C-12
Wetaskiwin D-12
Whitecourt C-11

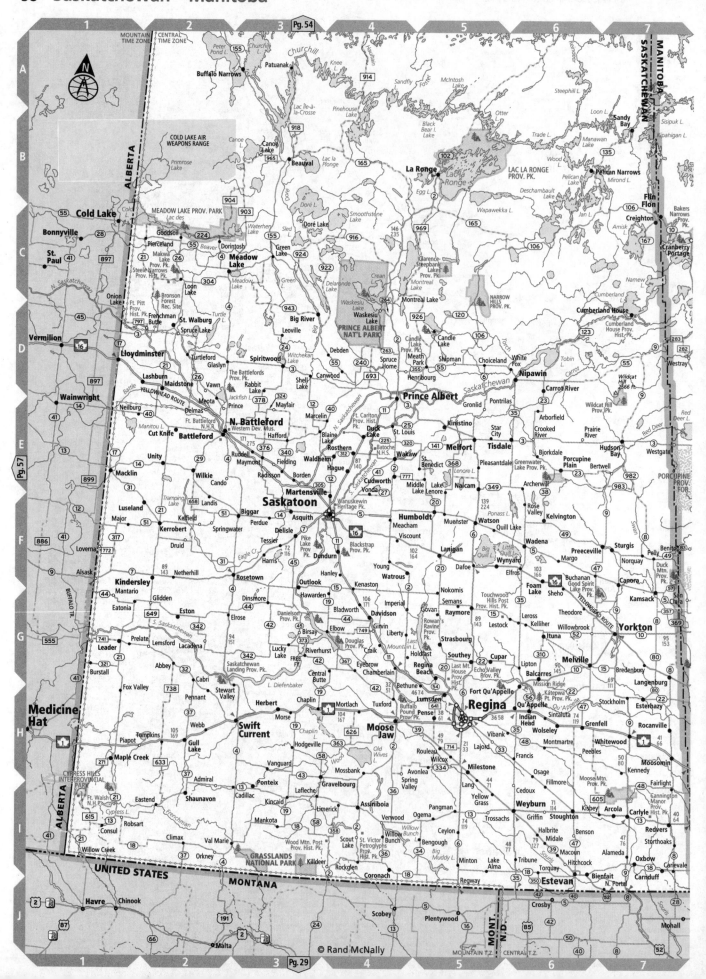

© Rand McNally

NOTE: Maps are not always in alphabetical order.
See Page 1 for map location in this atlas.

Saskatchewan • Manitoba 59

Saskatchewan
Population: 1,033,381
Land Area: 228,445 sq. mi.
Capital: Regina

Cities and Towns

Arcola I-7
Asquith F-3
Assiniboia I-4
Avonlea H-5
Balcarres G-6
Battleford E-2
Beauval B-3
Bethune G-5
Bienfait I-6
Big River D-3
Biggar F-3
Blaine Lake E-3
Buffalo Narrows A-3
Cabri G-2
Canora F-7
Canwood D-4
Carlyle I-7
Carnduff I-7
Carrot River D-6
Central Butte G-4
Choiceland D-5
Coronach I-4
Craik G-4
Creighton C-7
Cudworth E-4
Cumberland House D-7
Cupar G-5
Cut Knife E-2
Davidson G-4
Debden D-4
Delisle F-3
Duck Lake E-4
Dundurn F-4
Eastend I-2
Eatonia G-1
Elrose G-2
Esterhazy H-7
Estevan I-6
Eston G-2
Foam Lake F-6
Fort Qu'Appelle G-6
Glaslyn D-2
Gravelbourg H-3
Green Lake C-3
Grenfell H-6
Gull Lake H-2
Hafford E-3
Hague E-4
Hanley F-4
Herbert H-3
Hudson Bay E-7
Humboldt F-5
Indian Head H-6
Ituna G-6
Kamsack G-7
Kelvington F-6
Kerrobert F-2
Kindersley F-2
Kinistino E-5
La Ronge B-5
Lafleche I-3
Langenburg G-7
Lanigan F-5
Lashburn D-2
Leader G-1
Leoville D-3
Lloydminster D-1
Lucky Lake G-3
Lumsden H-5
Luseland F-2
Macklin E-1
Maidstone D-2
Maple Creek H-1
Martensville F-4
Meadow Lake C-2
Melfort E-5
Melville G-6
Midale I-6
Milestone H-5
Montmartre H-6
Moose Jaw H-4
Moosomin H-7
Muenster F-5
Naicam E-5
Neilburg E-1
Nipawin D-6
Nokomis G-5
Norquay F-7
North Battleford E-2
Outlook F-3
Oxbow I-7
Pelican Narrows B-6
Pense H-5
Perdue F-3
Pierceland C-2
Ponteix I-3
Porcupine Plain E-6
Preeceville F-7
Prince Albert D-4
Qu'Appelle H-6
Quill Lake F-5
Radisson E-3
Raymore G-5
Redvers I-7
Regina H-5
Regina Beach G-5
Rocanville H-7
Rockglen I-4
Rosetown F-3
Rosthern E-4
Rouleau H-5
Saint Louis E-4
Saint Walburg D-2
Sandy Bay B-7
Saskatoon F-4
Shaunavon I-2
Southey G-5
Spiritwood D-3
Star City E-5
Stoughton I-6
Strasbourg G-5
Sturgis F-7
Swift Current H-3
Theodore G-6
Tisdale E-5
Turtleford D-2
Unity E-2
Vibank H-6
Wadena F-6
Wakaw E-4
Waldheim E-4
Watrous F-5
Watson F-5
Weyburn I-5
White Fox D-6
Whitewood H-6
Wilkie E-2
Wolseley H-6
Wynyard F-5
Yellow Grass I-5
Yorkton G-7

Manitoba
Population: 1,208,268
Land Area: 213,729 sq. mi.
Capital: Winnipeg

Cities and Towns

Amaranth H-10
Angusville H-8
Arborg G-11
Ashern G-10
Austin H-9
Baldur I-9
Beausejour H-11
Belmont I-9
Benito F-7
Berens River E-11
Binscarth H-8
Birch River E-8
Birtle H-8
Boissevain I-9
Bowsman F-8
Brandon I-9
Camperville F-8
Carberry I-9
Carman I-10
Cartwright I-9
Cormorant C-8
Cranberry Portage C-7
Crystal City I-9
Darlingford I-10
Dauphin G-9
Deloraine I-8
Douglas H-9
Duck Bay F-8
Elkhorn H-8
Elm Creek H-10
Elphinstone H-8
Emerson I-11
Erickson H-9
Eriksdale G-10
Ethelbert G-8
Fisher Branch G-10
Flin Flon C-7
Gilbert Plains G-8
Gimli G-11
Gladstone H-9
Glenboro I-9
Glenella H-9
Grand Rapids E-9
Grandview G-8
Gretna I-11
Gypsumville F-10
Hamiota H-8
Hartney I-8
Holland I-9
Inglis G-8
Inwood H-11
Kenville F-8
Killarney I-9
La Broquerie I-11
Lac du Bonnet H-12
Langruth H-10
Letellier I-11
Lockport H-11
Lowe Farm I-10
Lundar G-10
MacGregor H-10
Mafeking E-8
Manigotagan G-11
Manitou I-10
Matheson Island F-11
McCreary G-9
Melita I-8
Miniota H-8
Minitonas F-8
Minnedosa H-9
Moose Lake D-8
Moosehorn G-10
Morden I-10
Morris I-11
Neepawa H-9
Newdale H-8
Ninette I-9
Niverville I-11
Norway House D-10
Oak River H-8
Oakburn H-8
Oakville H-10
Ochre River G-9
Petersfield H-11
Pierson I-8
Pilot Mound I-10
Pine Falls H-11
Pine River F-8
Pipestone I-8
Plum Coulee I-10
Plumas H-9
Poplar Point H-10
Portage la Prairie H-10
Rathwell H-10
Rennie H-12
Reston I-8
Richer I-11
Rivers H-8
Riverton G-11
Roblin G-8
Roland I-10
Rorketon G-9
Rossburn H-8
Russell G-8
Saint Claude I-10
Saint Jean Baptiste I-11
Saint Laurent H-10
Saint Malo I-11
Saint-Georges H-12
Sainte Agathe I-11
Sainte Anne I-11
Saint-Pierre-Jolys I-11
Sainte Rose du Lac G-9
Sanford I-11
Selkirk H-11
Shoal Lake H-8
Sifton G-8
Snow Lake B-8
Somerset I-10
Souris I-8
Sprague I-12
Steinbach I-11
Swan River F-8
Teulon H-11
The Pas A-10
Thompson A-10
Treherne I-10
Tyndall H-11
Victoria Beach G-11
Virden I-8
Vita I-11
Wabowden B-9
Warren H-11
Wawanesa I-9
Whitemouth H-12
Wilkie I-10
Winnipeg H-11
Winnipeg Beach H-11
Winnipegosis F-9
Woodridge I-12

Pg. 54
Pg. 61
Pg. 38
Pg. 26

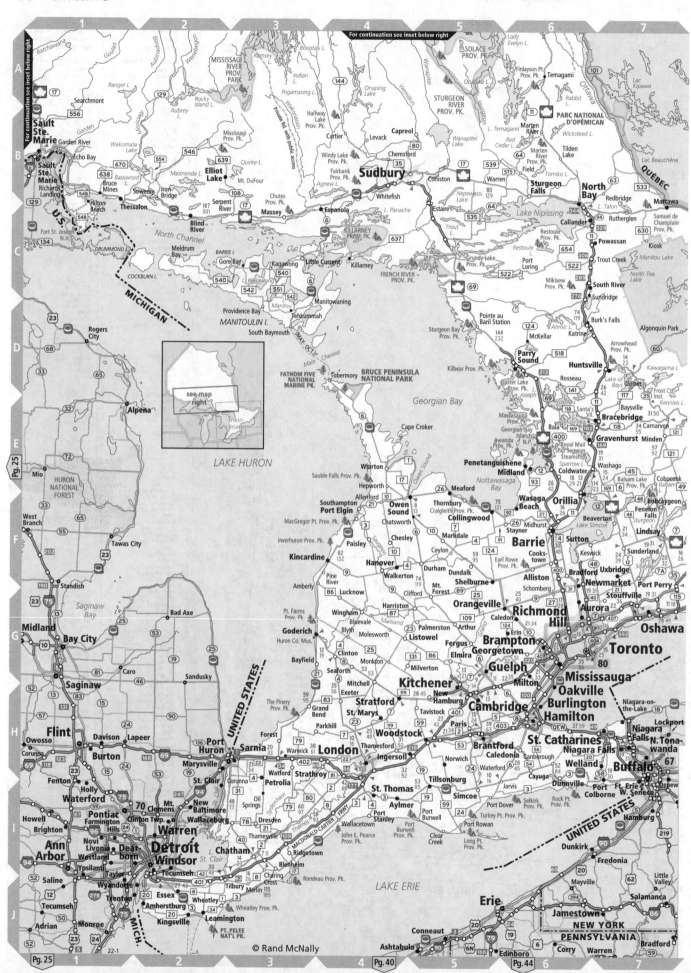

For continuation see inset below right

For continuation see inset below right

QUÉBEC

PARC NATIONAL D'OPÉMICAN

MICHIGAN

MANITOULIN I.

BRUCE PENINSULA NATIONAL PARK

FATHOM FIVE NATIONAL MARINE PK.

Georgian Bay

see map right

LAKE HURON

HURON NATIONAL FOREST

Sault Ste. Marie

Sudbury

North Bay

Elliot Lake

Parry Sound

Huntsville

Bracebridge

Gravenhurst

Orillia

Barrie

Owen Sound

Collingwood

Wasaga Beach

Lindsay

Kincardine

Hanover

Orangeville

Richmond Hill

Aurora

Oshawa

Toronto

Brampton

Mississauga

Oakville

Burlington

Hamilton

Guelph

Kitchener

Cambridge

Milton

Goderich

Listowel

Fergus

Stratford

Woodstock

Paris

Brantford

St. Catharines

Niagara Falls

London

Ingersoll

Tillsonburg

Simcoe

St. Thomas

Buffalo

Flint

Burton

Saginaw

Bay City

Midland

Sarnia

Port Huron

Detroit

Windsor

Chatham

Ann Arbor

Warren

Pontiac

LAKE ERIE

Erie

Jamestown

NEW YORK

PENNSYLVANIA

UNITED STATES

UNITED STATES

MICH.

© Rand McNally

NOTE: Maps are not always in alphabetical order.
See Page 1 for map location in this atlas.

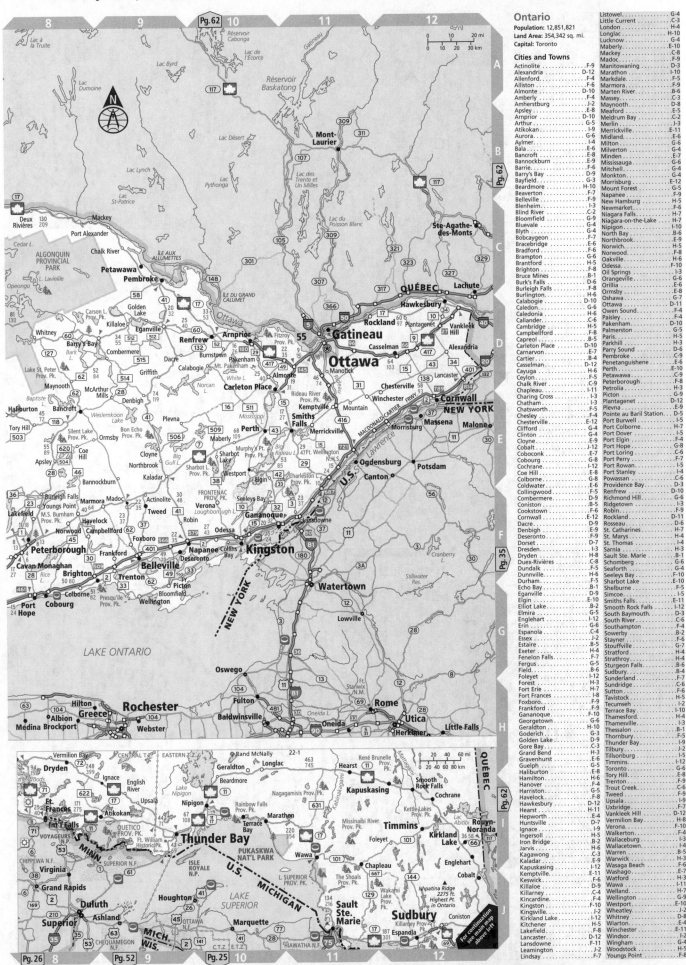

Ontario

Population: 12,851,821
Land Area: 354,342 sq. mi.
Capital: Toronto

Cities and Towns

Actinolite	F-9
Alexandria	D-12
Allenford	D-4
Alliston	F-6
Almonte	D-10
Amberly	F-4
Amherstburg	J-2
Apsley	E-8
Arnprior	D-10
Arthur	G-5
Atikokan	I-9
Aurora	G-6
Aylmer	I-4
Bala	E-7
Bancroft	E-8
Bannockburn	E-9
Barrie	F-6
Barry's Bay	D-9
Bayfield	G-3
Beardmore	H-10
Beaverton	F-7
Belleville	F-9
Blenheim	I-3
Blind River	C-2
Bloomfield	G-9
Bluevale	G-4
Blyth	G-4
Bobcaygeon	F-7
Bracebridge	E-6
Bradford	F-6
Brampton	G-6
Brantford	H-5
Brighton	F-8
Bruce Mines	B-1
Burk's Falls	D-6
Burleigh Falls	F-8
Burlington	H-6
Calabogie	D-10
Caledon	G-6
Caledonia	H-6
Callander	C-6
Cambridge	H-5
Campbellford	F-8
Capreol	B-5
Carleton Place	D-10
Carnarvon	E-7
Cartier	B-4
Casselman	D-12
Cayuga	H-6
Ceylon	F-5
Chalk River	C-9
Chapleau	I-11
Charing Cross	I-3
Chatham	I-3
Chatsworth	F-5
Chesley	F-4
Chesterville	E-12
Clifford	G-4
Clinton	G-4
Cloyne	D-9
Cobalt	I-12
Coboconk	E-7
Cobourg	G-8
Cochrane	I-12
Coe Hill	E-8
Colborne	G-8
Coldwater	E-6
Collingwood	F-5
Combermere	D-9
Coniston	B-5
Cookstown	F-6
Cornwall	E-12
Dacre	D-9
Denbigh	E-9
Deseronto	F-9
Dorset	D-7
Dresden	I-3
Dryden	H-8
Duex-Rivières	C-8
Dundalk	F-5
Dunnville	H-6
Durham	F-5
Echo Bay	B-1
Eganville	D-9
Elgin	E-10
Elliot Lake	B-2
Elmira	G-5
Englehart	I-12
Erin	G-6
Espanola	C-4
Essex	J-2
Estaire	B-5
Exeter	H-4
Fenelon Falls	F-7
Fergus	G-5
Field	B-6
Foleyet	I-12
Forest	H-3
Fort Erie	H-7
Fort Frances	I-8
Foxboro	F-9
Frankford	F-9
Gananoque	F-10
Georgetown	G-6
Geraldton	H-10
Goderich	G-3
Golden Lake	D-9
Gore Bay	C-3
Grand Bend	H-3
Gravenhurst	E-6
Guelph	G-5
Haliburton	E-8
Hamilton	H-6
Hanover	F-4
Harriston	G-5
Havelock	F-8
Hawkesbury	D-12
Hearst	H-11
Hepworth	E-4
Huntsville	D-7
Ignace	I-9
Ingersoll	H-5
Iron Bridge	B-2
Jarvis	H-6
Kagawong	C-3
Kaladar	E-9
Kapuskasing	I-12
Kemptville	E-11
Keswick	F-6
Killaloe	D-9
Killarney	C-4
Kincardine	F-4
Kingston	F-10
Kingsville	J-2
Kirkland Lake	I-12
Kitchener	H-5
Lakefield	F-8
Lancaster	D-12
Lansdowne	F-11
Leamington	J-2
Lindsay	F-7

Listowel	G-4
Little Current	C-3
London	H-4
Longlac	H-10
Lucknow	G-4
Maberly	E-10
Mackey	C-8
Madoc	F-9
Manitowaning	D-3
Marathon	I-10
Markdale	F-5
Marmora	F-9
Marten River	B-6
Massey	C-3
Maynooth	D-8
Meaford	E-5
Meldrum Bay	C-2
Merlin	J-3
Merrickville	E-11
Midland	E-6
Milton	G-6
Milverton	G-4
Minden	E-7
Mississauga	G-6
Mitchell	G-4
Monkton	G-4
Morrisburg	E-12
Mount Forest	G-5
Napanee	F-9
New Hamburg	H-5
Newmarket	F-6
Niagara Falls	H-7
Niagara-on-the-Lake	H-7
Nipigon	I-10
North Bay	B-6
Northbrook	E-9
Norwich	H-5
Norwood	F-8
Oakville	H-6
Odessa	F-10
Oil Springs	I-3
Orangeville	G-6
Orillia	E-6
Ormsby	E-8
Oshawa	G-7
Ottawa	D-11
Owen Sound	F-4
Paisley	F-4
Pakenham	D-10
Palmerston	G-5
Paris	H-5
Parkhill	H-3
Parry Sound	D-6
Pembroke	C-9
Penetanguishene	E-6
Perth	E-10
Petawawa	C-9
Peterborough	F-8
Petrolia	H-3
Picton	G-9
Plantagenet	D-12
Plevna	E-9
Pointe au Baril Station	D-5
Port Burwell	I-5
Port Colborne	H-6
Port Dover	I-5
Port Elgin	F-4
Port Hope	G-8
Port Loring	C-6
Port Perry	F-7
Port Rowan	I-5
Port Stanley	I-4
Powassan	C-6
Providence Bay	D-3
Renfrew	D-10
Richmond Hill	G-6
Ridgetown	I-3
Robin	F-9
Rockland	D-11
Rosseau	D-6
St. Catharines	H-7
St. Marys	H-4
St. Thomas	I-4
Sarnia	H-3
Sault Ste. Marie	B-1
Schomberg	G-6
Seaforth	G-4
Seeleys Bay	F-10
Sharbot Lake	E-10
Shelburne	F-5
Simcoe	I-5
Smiths Falls	E-11
Smooth Rock Falls	I-12
South Baymouth	D-3
South River	C-6
Southampton	F-4
Sowerby	B-2
Stayner	F-6
Stouffville	G-7
Stratford	H-4
Strathroy	H-4
Sturgeon Falls	B-6
Sudbury	B-4
Sunderland	F-7
Sundridge	C-6
Sutton	F-6
Tavistock	H-5
Tecumseh	I-2
Terrace Bay	I-10
Thamesford	H-4
Thamesville	I-3
Thessalon	B-2
Thornbury	F-5
Thunder Bay	I-9
Tilbury	I-3
Tillsonburg	I-5
Timmins	I-12
Toronto	G-6
Tory Hill	E-8
Trenton	F-9
Trout Creek	C-6
Tweed	F-9
Upsala	H-9
Uxbridge	F-7
Vankleek Hill	D-12
Vermilion Bay	H-8
Verona	F-10
Walkerton	F-4
Wallaceburg	I-3
Wallacetown	I-4
Warren	B-5
Warwick	H-3
Wasaga Beach	F-6
Washago	E-7
Watford	H-3
Wawa	I-11
Welland	H-7
Wellington	G-9
Westport	E-10
Wheatley	J-2
Whitney	D-8
Wiarton	E-4
Winchester	E-11
Windsor	J-2
Wingham	G-4
Woodstock	H-5
Youngs Point	F-8

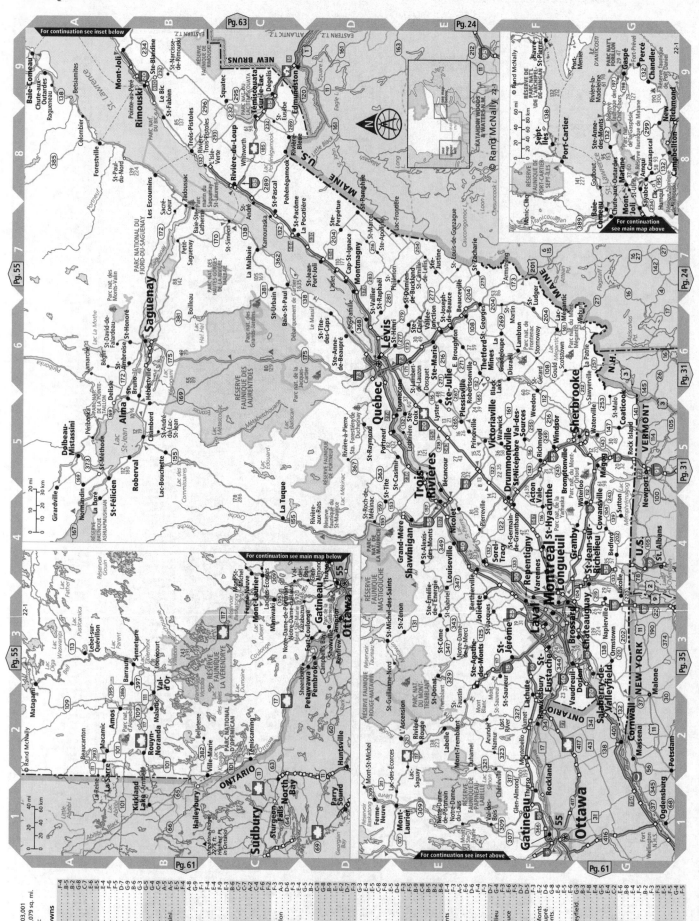

NOTE: Maps are not always in alphabetical order.
See Page 1 for map location in this atlas.

Atlantic Provinces 63

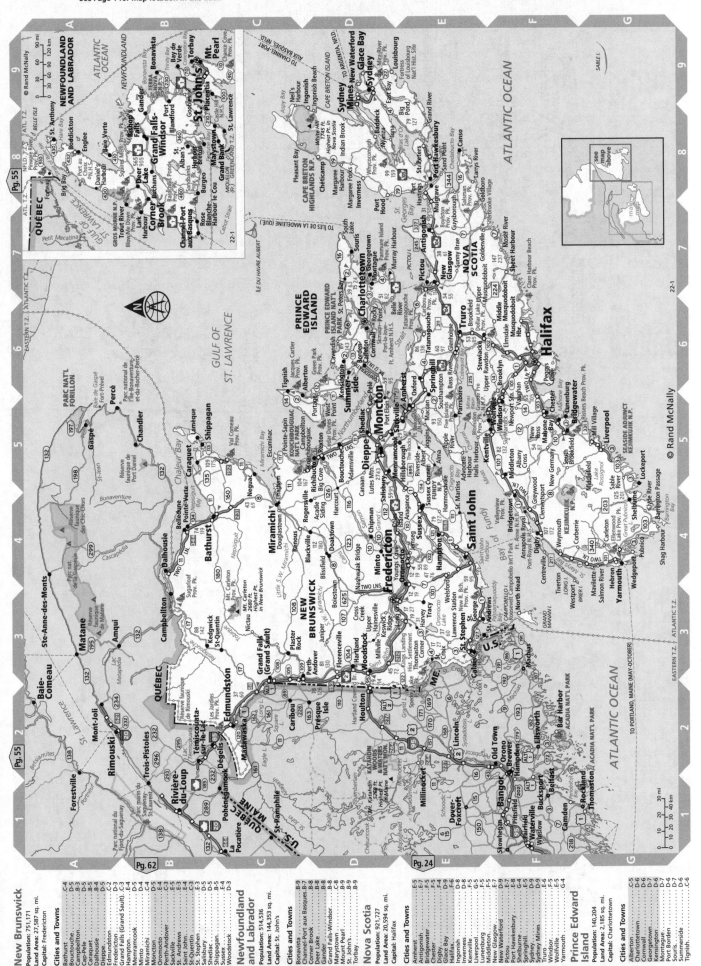

New Brunswick

Population: 751,171
Land Area: 27,587 sq. mi.
Capital: Fredericton

Cities and Towns

Bathurst	C-4
Boctouche	D-5
Campbellton	B-3
Cap-Pele	D-5
Caraquet	B-5
Dalhousie	B-4
Dieppe	D-5
Edmundston	C-2
Fredericton	C-4
Grand Falls (Grand Sault)	C-3
Hampton	D-5
Memramcook	D-5
Minto	D-4
Miramichi	C-4
Moncton	D-5
Oromocto	C-4
Perth-Andover	C-3
Sackville	D-5
Saint John	D-4
St. Andrews	E-4
St. Stephen	E-4
St. Quentin	C-3
Salisbury	D-5
Shediac	D-5
Shippagan	B-5
Sussex	D-5
Woodstock	D-3

Newfoundland and Labrador

Population: 514,536
Land Area: 144,353 sq. mi.
Capital: St. John's

Cities and Towns

Bonavista	B-9
Channel-Port aux Basques	B-7
Corner Brook	B-8
Deer Lake	B-8
Gander	B-8
Grand Falls-Windsor	B-8
Marystown	B-8
Mount Pearl	B-9
St. John's	B-9
Torbay	B-9

Nova Scotia

Population: 921,727
Land Area: 20,594 sq. mi.
Capital: Halifax

Cities and Towns

Amherst	E-5
Antigonish	D-8
Bridgewater	F-5
Chester	F-6
Digby	F-4
Glace Bay	D-9
Halifax	F-6
Ingonish	C-8
Inverness	D-8
Kentville	E-5
Liverpool	F-5
Lunenburg	F-6
Middleton	E-5
New Glasgow	D-7
New Waterford	D-9
Pictou	D-7
Port Hawkesbury	D-8
Shelburne	G-5
Springhill	E-6
Sydney	D-9
Sydney Mines	D-9
Truro	E-6
Windsor	E-5
Wolfville	E-5
Yarmouth	G-4

Prince Edward Island

Population: 140,204
Land Area: 2,185 sq. mi.
Capital: Charlottetown

Cities and Towns

Alberton	C-5
Charlottetown	D-6
Cornwall	D-6
Georgetown	D-7
Kensington	D-6
Montague	D-6
Port Borden	D-6
Souris	D-7
Summerside	D-6
Tignish	C-6

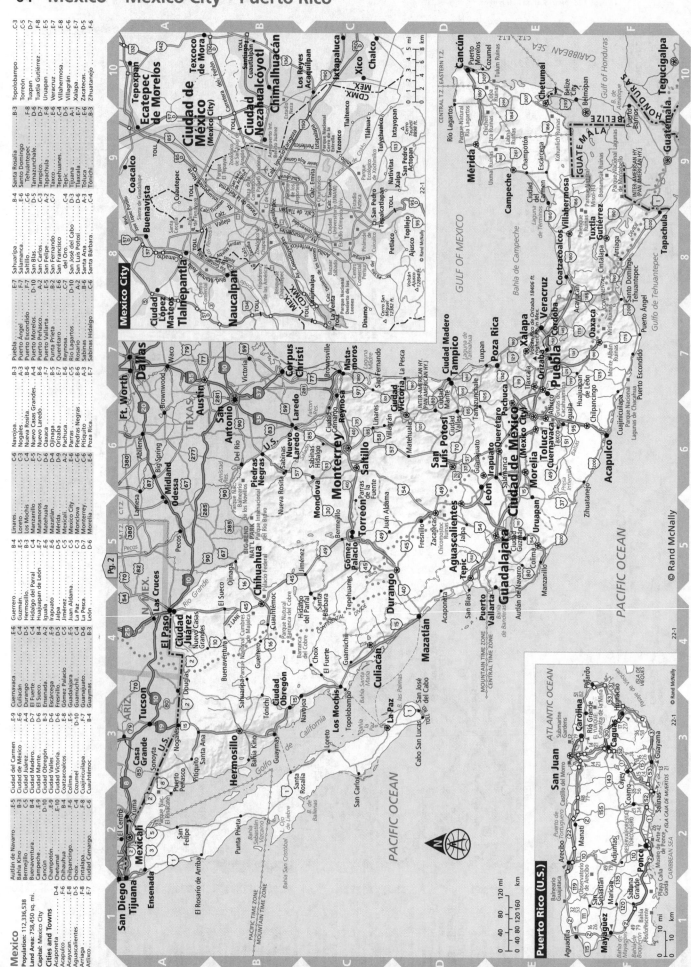

Mexico

Population: 112,336,538
Land Area: 758,450 sq. mi.
Capital: Mexico City

Cities and Towns

Acaponeta	D-4
Acapulco	F-6
Acayucan	E-8
Aguascalientes	D-5
Arriaga	E-8
Atlixco	E-7

Autlán de Navarro	E-5
Bahía Kino	B-3
Bermejillo	C-5
Buenaventura	B-4
Campeche	E-9
Cancún	D-10
Champotón	D-9
Chetumal	E-10
Chihuahua	B-4
Chilpancingo	F-6
Choix	B-3
Cintalapa	F-8
Ciudad Camargo	C-5

Ciudad del Carmen	E-9
Ciudad de México	E-6
Ciudad Juárez	A-4
Ciudad Madero	D-7
Ciudad Mante	D-6
Ciudad Obregón	B-3
Ciudad Valles	D-6
Ciudad Victoria	D-6
Coatzacoalcos	E-8
Colima	E-5
Cozumel	D-10
Cuajinicuilapa	F-7
Cuauhtémoc	B-4

Cuernavaca	E-6
Culiacán	C-3
Durango	C-4
El Fuerte	B-3
El Sueco	B-4
Ensenada	A-2
Escárcega	E-9
Fresnillo	C-5
Gómez Palacio	C-5
Guadalajara	E-5
Guamúchil	C-3
Guanajuato	E-6
Guaymas	B-3

Guerrero	E-6
Hermosillo	B-3
Hidalgo del Parral	C-4
Huajuapan de León	E-7
Iguala	E-6
Irapuato	E-6
Jalpa	D-5
Jiménez	C-5
Juan Aldama	C-5
La Paz	C-3
La Pesca	D-7
León	D-6

Linares	C-6
Loreto	C-3
Los Mochis	B-3
Manzanillo	E-5
Matamoros	D-6
Matehuala	D-6
Mazatlán	C-4
Mérida	D-9
Mexicali	A-2
Mexico City	E-6
Monclova	C-5
Monterrey	C-6
Morelia	E-6

Navojoa	B-3
Nogales	A-3
Nueva Rosita	C-5
Nuevo Casas Grandes	A-4
Nuevo Laredo	C-6
Oaxaca	F-7
Ojinaga	B-4
Orizaba	E-7
Parras	C-5
Pachuca	E-6
Piedras Negras	C-5
Pitiquito	A-3
Poza Rica	E-6

Puebla	E-7
Puerto Ángel	F-7
Puerto Escondido	F-7
Puerto Peñasco	A-2
Puerto Vallarta	D-4
Punta Prieta	B-2
Querétaro	E-6
Reynosa	C-7
Río Lagartos	D-10
Rosario	C-4
Sabinas	C-5
Sabinas Hidalgo	C-6

Sahuaripa	B-3
Salamanca	E-6
Saltillo	C-5
San Carlos	D-17
San Felipe	A-2
San Fernando	D-6
San Francisco	C-4
del Oro	
San José del Cabo	C-4
San Luis Potosí	D-6
Santa Ana	A-3
Santa Bárbara	C-4

Santa Rosalía	B-2
Santo Domingo	C-3
Tehuantepec	F-8
Tampico	D-7
Tapachula	F-8
Taxco	E-6
Tepic	D-4
Tepehuanes	C-4
Tijuana	A-1
Tlaxcala	E-7
Toluca	E-6
Tónichi	B-3

Topolobampo	C-3
Torreón	C-5
Tuxpan	D-7
Tuxtla Gutiérrez	F-8
Uruapan	E-5
Veracruz	E-8
Villahermosa	E-8
Villagrán	C-6
Xalapa	E-7
Zacatecas	D-5
Zihuatanejo	F-6

Mexico City

Puerto Rico (U.S.)

© Rand McNally

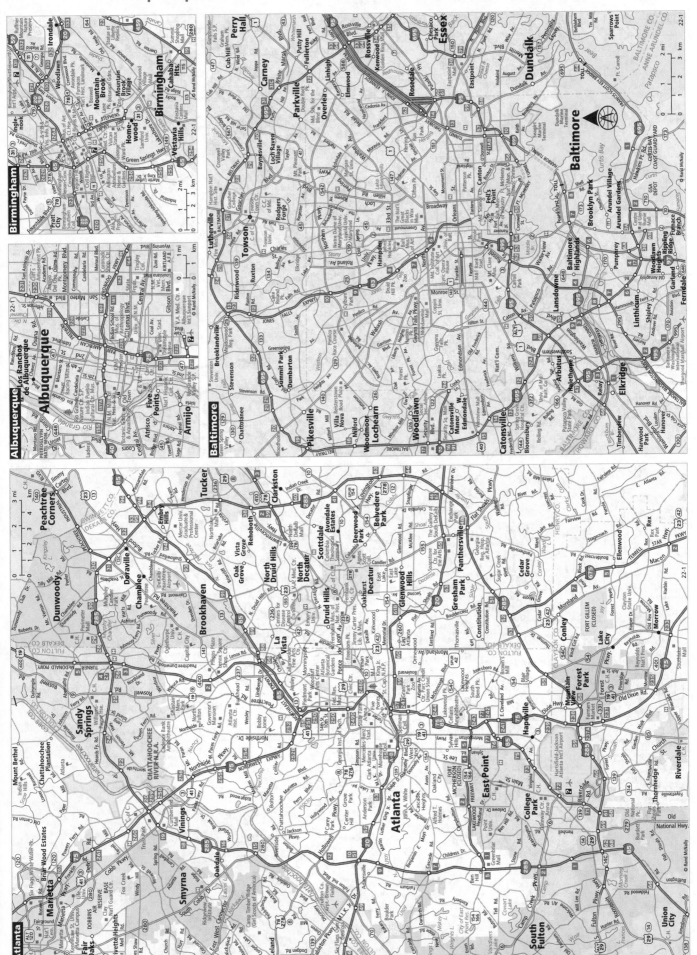

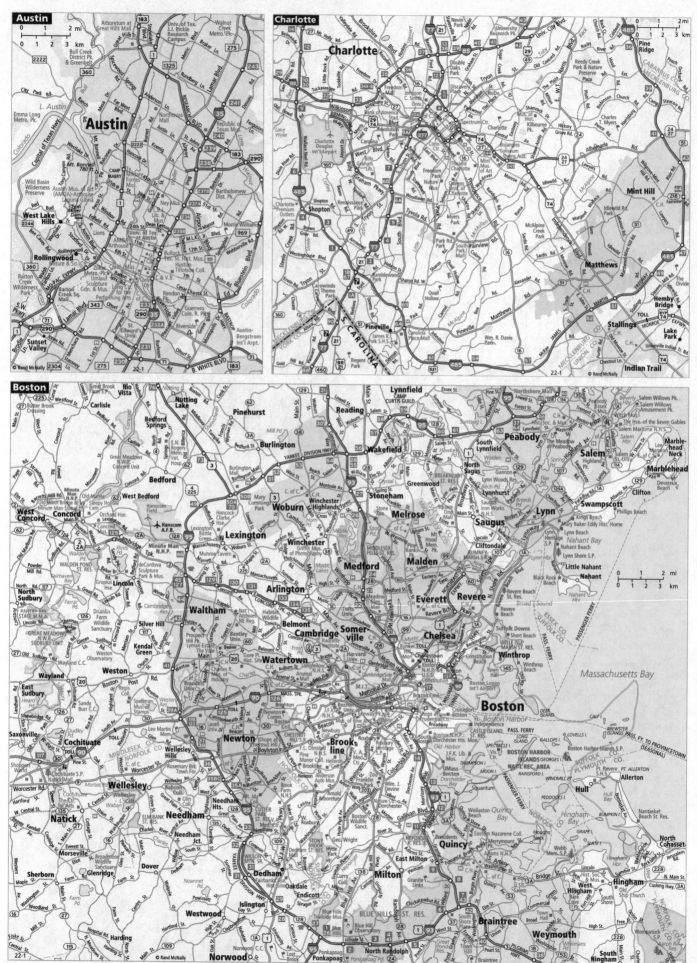

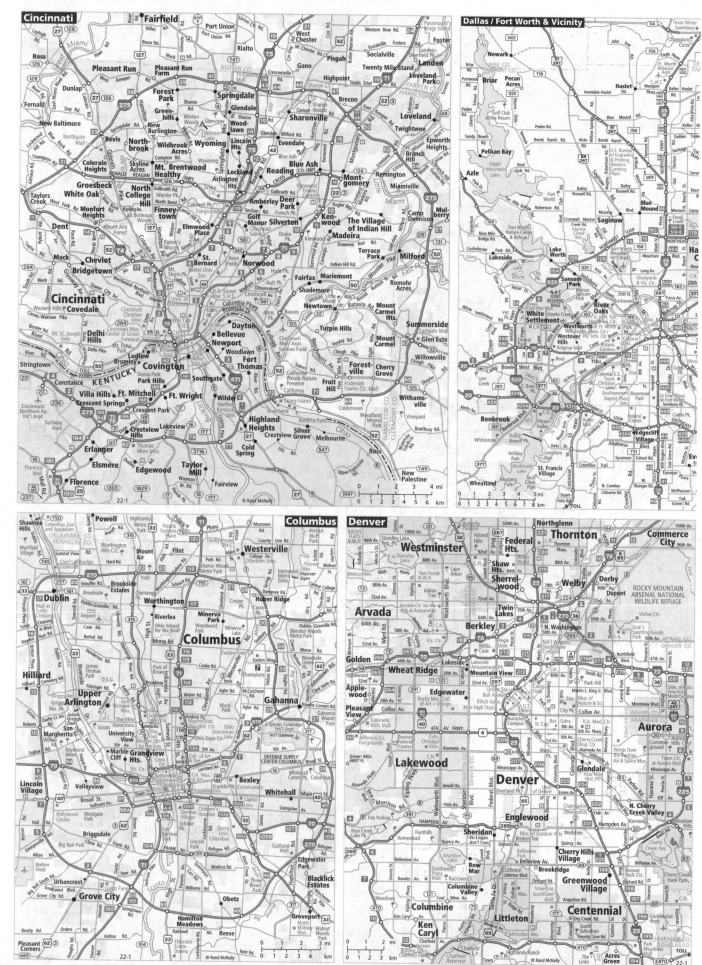

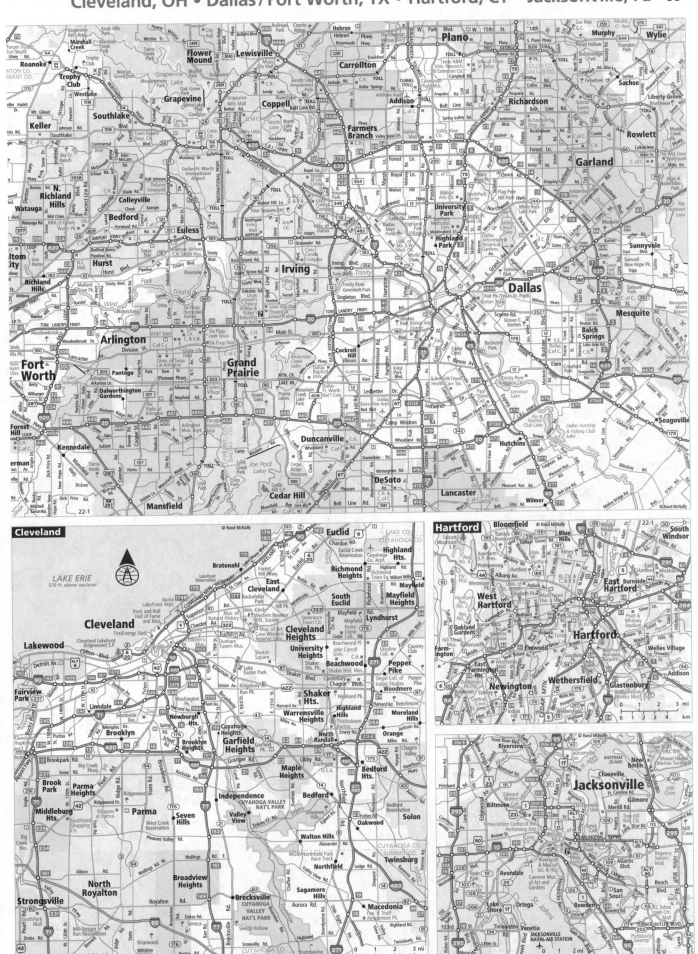

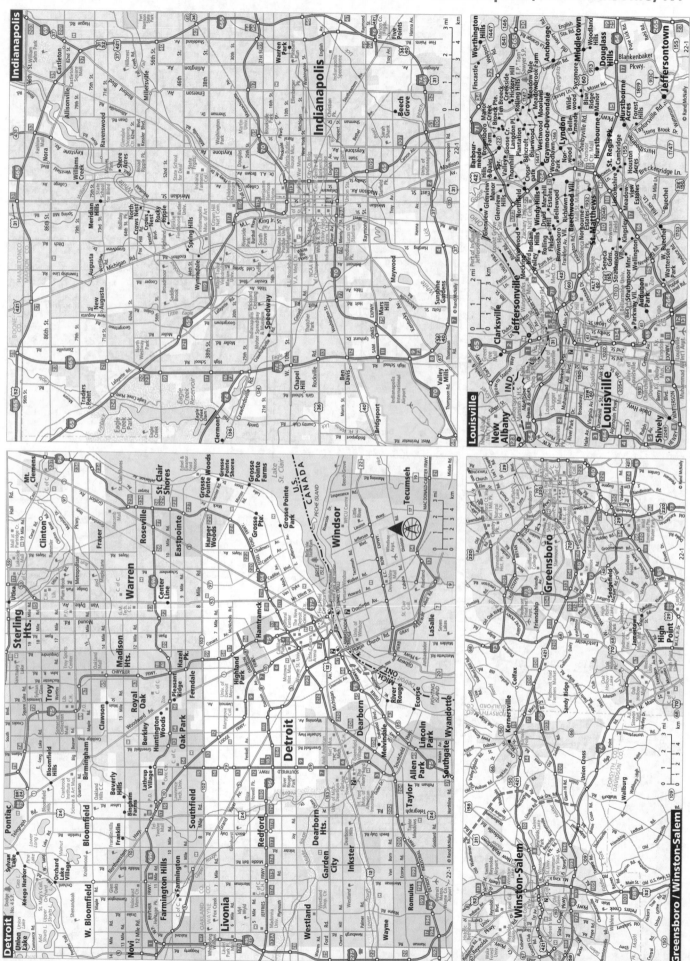

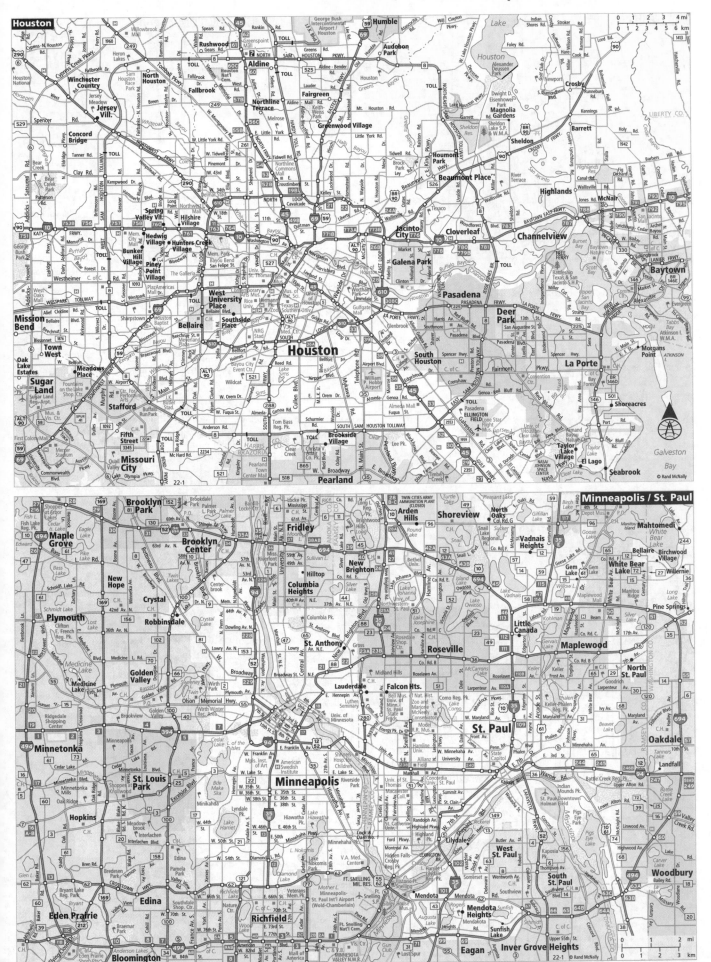

© Rand McNally

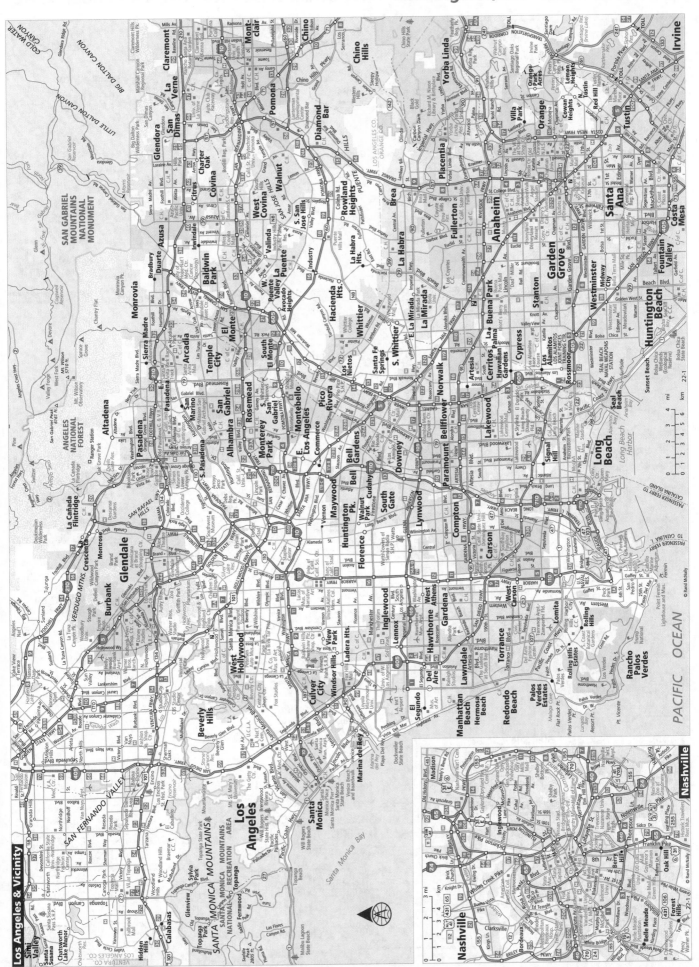

Nashville

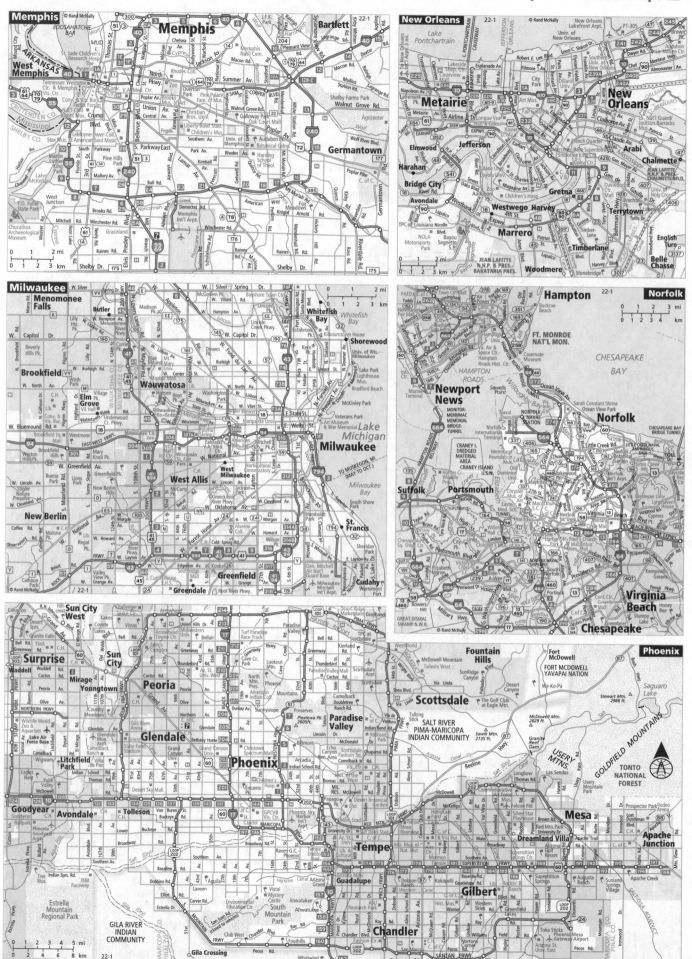

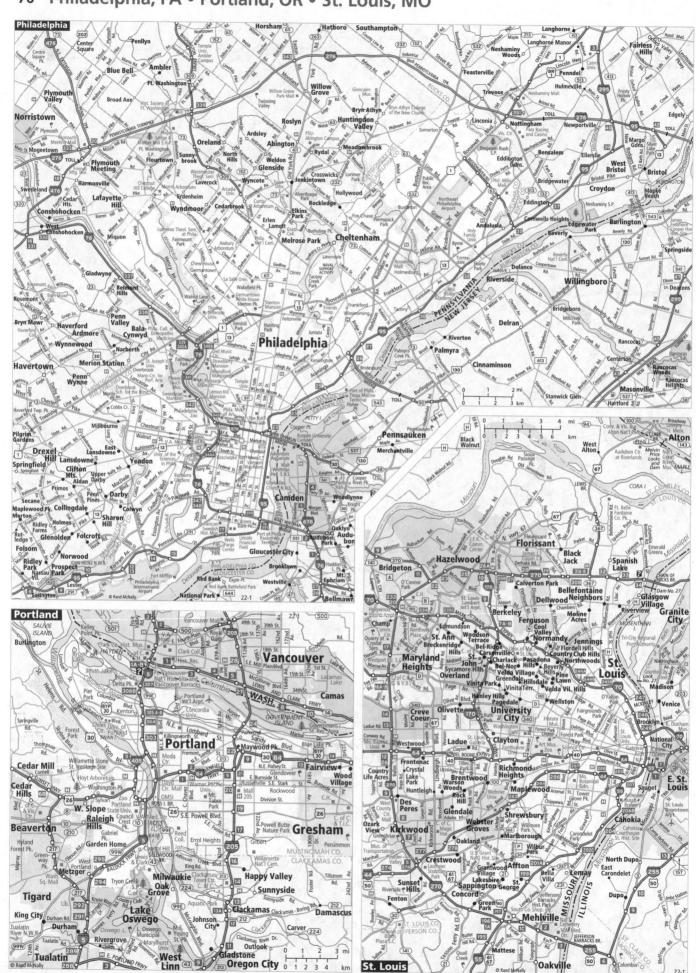

Philadelphia

Portland

St. Louis

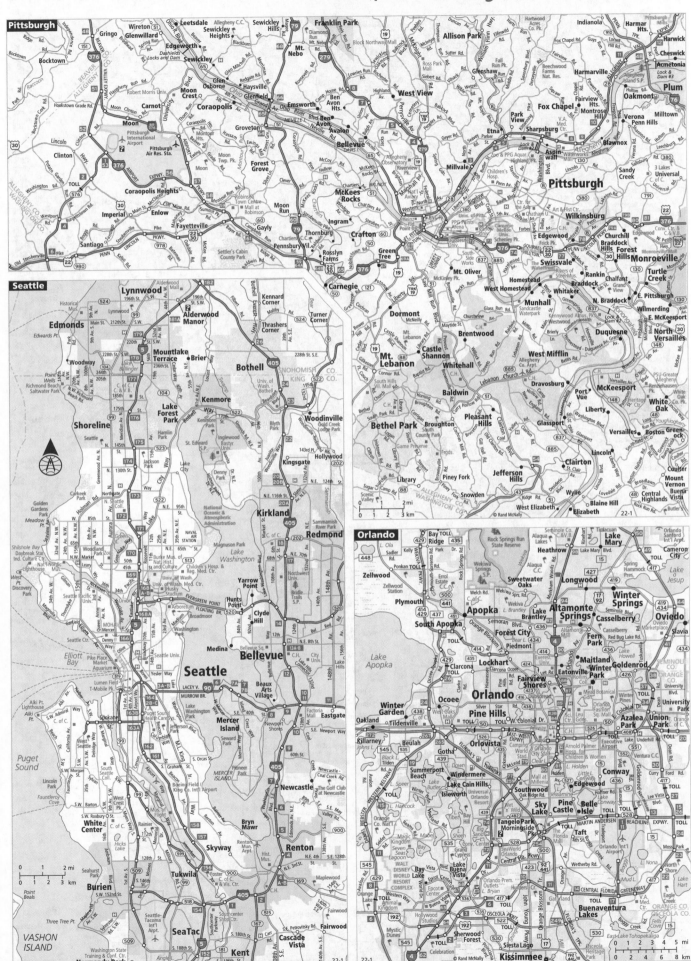

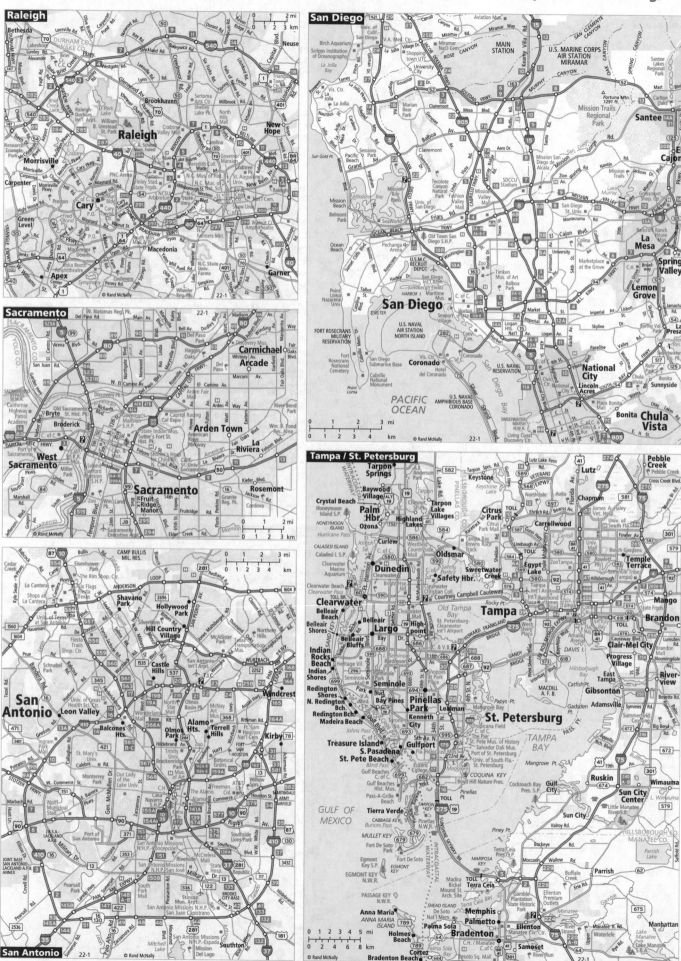

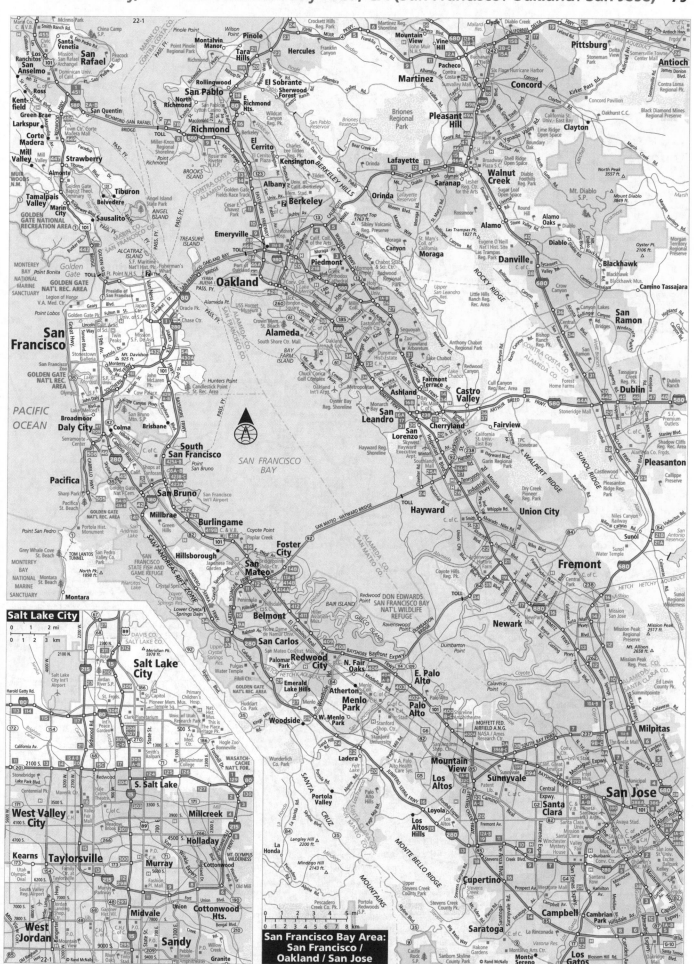

San Francisco Bay Area:
San Francisco /
Oakland / San Jose

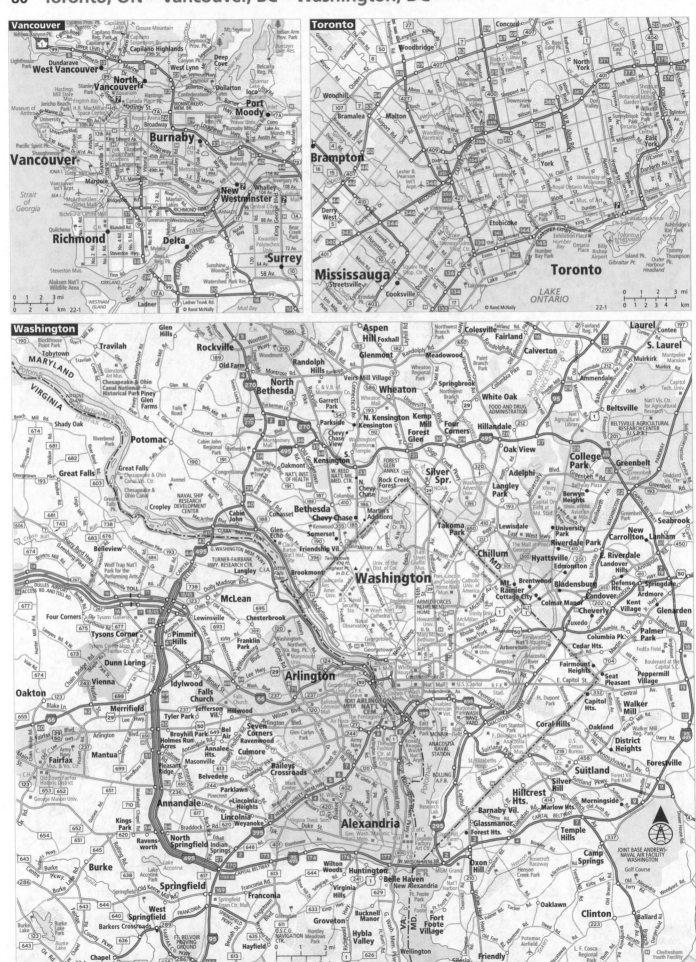

Hotel Resources

Best Western Hotels & Resorts
(800) 780-7234
www.bestwestern.com

Budget Host
(800) 283-4678
www.budgethost.com

Choice Hotels
(877) 424-6423
www.choicehotels.com

Ascend Hotel Collection
www.choicehotels.com/ascend

Cambria Hotels
www.choicehotels.com/cambria

Clarion & Clarion Pointe Hotels
www.choicehotels.com/clarion
www.choicehotels.com/
clarion-pointe

Comfort Inn & Comfort Suites
www.choicehotels.com/
comfort-inn
www.choicehotels.com/
comfort-suites

EconoLodge
www.choicehotels.com/
econo-lodge

MainStay Suites
www.choicehotels.com/mainstay

Quality Inn Hotels
www.choicehotels.com/
quality-inn

Rodeway Inn
www.choicehotels.com/
rodeway-inn

Sleep Inn
www.choicehotels.com/sleep-inn

Woodspring Suites
(844) 974-6835
www.woodspring.com

Coast Hotels & Resorts
(800) 716-6199
www.coasthotels.com

Drury Hotels
(800) 378-7946
www.druryhotels.com

Extended Stay America
(800) 804-3724
www.extendedstayamerica.com

Fairmont
(800) 257-7544
www.fairmont.com

Four Seasons
(800) 819-5053
www.fourseasons.com

Hilton
(800) 445-8667
www.hilton.com

Canopy
(844) 692-2667
www.hilton.com/en/canopy

Conrad Hotels & Resorts
(800) 266-7237
www.hilton.com/en/conrad

Doubletree
(855) 610-8733
www.hilton.com/en/doubletree

Embassy Suites
(800) 362-2779
www.hilton.com/en/embassy

Hampton Inn
(800) 426-7866
www.hilton.com/en/hampton

Homewood Suites by Hilton
(800) 225-5466
www.hilton.com/en/homewood

Hyatt Hotels & Resorts
(800) 233-1234
www.hyatt.com

Intercontinental Hotels Group
(888) 424-6835
www.intercontinental.com

Candlewood Suites
(877) 226-3539
www.ihg.com/candlewood

Crowne Plaza Hotel & Resorts
(877) 227-6963
www.crowneplaza.com

Holiday Inn & Holiday Inn Express
(888) 465-4329
www.holidayinn.com

Hotel Indigo
(877) 846-3446
www.hotelindigo.com

Kimpton Hotels
(800) 546-7866
www.ihg.com/kimptonhotels

Staybridge Suites
(877) 238-8889
www.staybridge.com

Loews Hotels
(800) 235-6397
www.loewshotels.com

Marriott Bonvoy
(800) 228-9290
www.marriott.com
jw-marriott.marriott.com

Aloft Hotels
(877) 462-5638
aloft-hotels.marriott.com

Courtyard by Marriott
(800) 321-2211
courtyard.marriott.com

Delta Hotels & Resorts
(888) 890-3222
deltahotels.marriott.com

Fairfield
(800) 228-2800
fairfield.marriott.com

Four Points by Sheraton
(800) 368-7764
four-points.marriott.com

Gaylord Hotels
(800) 429-5673
www.marriott.com/
gaylord-hotels/travel.mi

Le Méridien Hotels & Resorts
(800) 543-4300
le-meridien.marriott.com

Renaissance Hotels
(800) 468-3571
renaissance-hotels.marriott.com

Residence Inn
(800) 331-3131
residence-inn.marriott.com

The Ritz-Carlton
(800) 241-3333
www.ritzcarlton.com

Sheraton Hotels & Resorts
(800) 325-3535
sheraton.marriott.com

St. Regis
(877) 787-3447
st-regis.marriott.com

W Hotels
(877) 946-8357
w-hotels.marriott.com

Westin Hotels & Resorts
(800) 937-8461
westin.marriott.com

Motel 6
(800) 899-9841
www.motel6.com

Omni Hotels & Resorts
(888) 444-6664
www.omnihotels.com

Preferred Hotels & Resorts
(866) 990-9491
legacy.preferredhotels.com

Radisson Hotel Group
(800) 333-3333 (U.S.)
(866) 434-2824 (Canada)
www.radissonhotels.com/en-us

Red Lion
(800) 733-5466
www.redlion.com

America's Best Value Inn
www.redlion.com/
americas-best-value-inn

Guesthouse
www.redlion.com/guesthouse

Hotel RL
www.redlion.com/hotel-rl

Knights Inn
www.redlion.com/knights-inn

Lexington Hotels & Inns
www.redlion.com/
lexington-hotels-inns

Signature Inn
www.redlion.com/signature-inn

Red Roof Inn
(877) 843-7663
www.redroof.com

Wyndham
(877) 999-3223
www.wyndhamhotels.com

AmericInn
(800) 634-3444
www.wyndhamhotels.com/
americinn

Baymont
(800) 337-0550
www.wyndhamhotels.com/
baymont

Days Inn
(800) 225-3297
www.wyndhamhotels.com/
days-inn

Dolce
(800) 983-6523
www.wyndhamhotels.com/dolce

Howard Johnson
(800) 221-5801
www.wyndhamhotels.com/hojo

La Quinta
(800) 753-3757
www.wyndhamhotels.com/
laquinta

Microtel
(800) 337-0050
www.wyndhamhotels.com/
microtel

Ramada
(800) 854-9517
www.wyndhamhotels.com/
ramada

Super 8
(800) 454-3213
www.wyndhamhotels.com/
super-8

Travelodge
(800) 525-4055
www.wyndhamhotels.com/
travelodge

TRYP
(800) 422-1115
www.wyndhamhotels.com/tryp

Wingate
(800) 337-0077
www.wyndhamhotels.com/
wingate

Wyndham Garden
(877) 999-3223
www.wyndhamhotels.com/
wyndham-garden

NOTE: All toll-free reservation numbers are for the U.S. and Canada unless otherwise noted. These numbers were accurate at press time but are subject to change.

Mileage Chart

This handy chart offers more than 2,400 mileages covering 77 North American cities. Want more mileages? Visit randmcnally.com/MC and type in any two cities or addresses.

	Albuquerque, NM	Atlanta, GA	Billings, MT	Boston, MA	Charlotte, NC	Chicago, IL	Cincinnati, OH	Dallas, TX	Denver, CO	Detroit, MI	Houston, TX	Indianapolis, IN	Kansas City, MO	Los Angeles, CA	Memphis, TN	Miami, FL	Milwaukee, WI	Minneapolis, MN	New Orleans, LA	New York, NY	Omaha, NE	Orlando, FL	Philadelphia, PA	Phoenix, AZ	Pittsburgh, PA	Portland, OR	St. Louis, MO	Salt Lake City, UT	San Francisco, CA	Seattle, WA	Washington, DC	Wichita, KS
Albuquerque, NM		1386	998	2219	1626	1333	1387	647	446	1570	884	1279	784	786	1008	1952	1354	1225	1165	2001	863	1730	1924	425	1641	1363	1037	599	1086	1438	1885	591
Amarillo, TX	288	1102	965	1935	1342	1049	1103	363	424	1586	589	995	570	1072	720	1668	1132	1009	881	1716	647	1446	1640	746	1357	1669	752	883	1370	1743	1600	418
Atlanta, GA	1386		1831	1095	244	715	461	780	1404	722	794	533	800	2174	379	661	809	1127	468	882	992	440	780	1844	684	2603	555	1878	2472	2649	637	955
Atlantic City, NJ	1985	831	2072	338	590	818	632	1518	1792	644	1598	703	1187	2774	1063	1248	910	1232	1273	126	1272	1038	60	2447	365	2922	948	2201	2934	2889	188	1379
Austin, TX	705	920	1495	1959	1164	1121	1128	196	950	1358	163	1067	702	1381	643	1341	1204	1136	503	1737	839	1124	1658	1010	1411	2068	825	1304	1760	2143	1524	542
Baltimore, MD	1887	683	1953	400	442	699	513	1368	1673	524	1448	584	1068	2670	914	1082	792	1112	1124	192	1153	889	97	2349	246	2804	829	2081	2816	2771	39	1260
Billings, MT	998	1831		2236	1990	1246	1546	1425	551	1535	1652	1435	1026	1240	1477	2497	1173	838	1868	2041	845	2275	2011	1210	1713	891	1278	552	1173	818	1951	1064
Birmingham, AL	1241	146	1780	1177	390	660	466	636	1329	724	668	478	749	2030	233	746	754	1072	343	960	939	534	880	1700	748	2551	502	1826	2327	2598	745	810
Boise, ID	938	2177	621	2660	2336	1693	1943	1702	830	1960	1930	1835	1372	842	1825	2844	1732	1461	2216	2465	1225	2622	2435	914	2137	431	1622	340	639	503	2375	1338
Boston, MA	2219	1095	2236		841	983	870	1764	1970	724	1844	937	1421	2983	1312	1482	1074	1396	1520	216	1436	1288	306	2681	570	3086	1182	2365	3098	3054	439	1613
Branson, MO	864	652	1241	1433	868	545	601	435	806	784	602	493	209	1651	274	1284	630	643	597	1201	402	1062	1138	1326	851	2013	249	1288	1950	2060	1081	292
Calgary, AB	1542	2357	541	2615	2400	1627	1925	1967	1096	1916	2209	1814	1567	1557	2028	3018	1555	1221	2419	2439	1387	2791	2454	2093	1787	1820	869		1500	678	2334	1606
Charleston, SC	1703	319	2133	970	209	908	620	1099	1706	826	1105	726	1103	2491	696	583	1002	1324	742	768	1294	380	668	2165	654	2904	857	2180	2789	2951	532	1272
Charlotte, NC	1626	244	1990	841		769	477	1023	1566	616	1038	583	961	2414	619	728	867	1180	712	641	1151	526	539	2088	446	2761	714	2037	2712	2808	398	1092
Chicago, IL	1333	715	1246	983	769		289	926	1002	282	1085	181	526	2015	531	1381	90	408	923	787	470	1153	757	1795	459	2118	295	1398	2130	2063	697	724
Cincinnati, OH	1387	461	1546	870	477	289		942	1187	259	1055	109	584	2172	482	1127	381	703	804	637	722	905	571	1849	288	2369	348	1647	2380	2363	512	779
Cleveland, OH	1598	714	1597	638	514	344	248	1194	1330	169	1315	315	799	2342	729	1240	434	756	1057	460	797	1043	428	2060	134	2446	560	1725	2458	2414	370	992
Columbus, OH	1457	567	1606	763	426	354	107	1039	1261	212	1174	189	657	2244	587	1164	445	766	910	533	792	954	468	1920	174	2439	421	1718	2451	2425	411	851
Corpus Christi, TX	855	1001	1622	2051	1244	1338	1262	410	1077	1542	207	1228	919	1494	782	1394	1421	1353	554	1844	1056	1172	1754	1122	1561	2218	1042	1454	1873	2292	1619	758
Dallas, TX	647	780	1425	1764	1023	926	934		880	1163	239	873	489	1437	453	1307	1010	928	519	1548	656	1086	1467	1066	1221	2128	630	1403	1734	2193	1332	361
Denver, CO	446	1404	551	1970	1566	1002	1187	880		1270	1035	1083	603	1015	1097	2069	1042	913	1398	1775	534	1851	1732	908	1447	1256	854	533	1268	1320	1671	519
Des Moines, IA	983	902	946	1299	1057	335	580	683	670	599	938	474	194	1682	617	1567	375	244	1008	1105	135	1339	1074	1445	777	1786	350	1065	1798	1764	1015	391
Detroit, MI	1570	722	1535	724	616	282	259	1163	1270		1319	277	764	2281	742	1354	374	696	1066	613	736	1144	583	2032	285	2385	533	1664	2397	2353	522	964
Duluth, MN	1375	1187	860	1370	1239	466	760	1092	1063	754	1331	651	586	2076	963	1852	394	152	1354	1264	530	1632	1230	1838	932	1749	679	1458	2033	1677	1171	785
Edmonton, AB	1724	2391	722	2549	2443	1670	1968	2149	1278	1958	2391	1857	1626	1755	2147	3058	1598	1264	2538	2482	1445	2836	2434	1721	2136	966	1878	1069	1695	793	2377	1787
El Paso, TX	266	1418	1257	2373	1662	1455	1569	635	707	1702	744	1398	929	796	1089	1934	1497	1347	1095	2202	1014	1712	2102	424	1797	1630	1157	866	1175	1705	1967	730
Fargo, ND	1318	1361	607	1629	1414	641	937	1079	873	930	1321	825	600	1848	1054	2025	569	234	1445	1438	420	1807	1405	1780	1107	1497	841	1160	1781	1424	1348	685
Gatlinburg, TN	1439	196	1803	922	202	578	290	884	1376	552	964	396	773	2226	431	865	672	994	640	707	964	640	625	1901	493	2574	527	1850	2525	2621	490	905
Guadalajara, JA	1194	1739	2194	2789	1982	1954	1962	1028	1639	2191	948	1901	1535	1501	1482	2131	2037	1969	1292	2592	1672	1910	2492	1212	2261	2545	1658	1792	1963	2631	2356	1377
Gulfport, MS	1221	399	1912	1482	643	896	767	562	1386	1025	403	780	883	1949	365	792	988	1196	78	1266	1073	572	1180	1577	1052	2633	647	1909	2307	2730	1036	867
Houston, TX	884	794	1652	1844	1038	1085	1055	239	1035	1319		1021	732	1550	575	1186	1163	1171	348	1632	898	965	1547	1178	1354	2356	784	1634	1929	2431	1411	595
Indianapolis, IN	1279	533	1435	937	583	181	109	873	1083	277	1021		482	2068	464	1198	272	591	818	707	613	968	643	1742	359	2260	243	1541	2273	2253	582	674
Jacksonville, FL	1636	346	2183	1146	379	1068	796	992	1756	1002	871	874	1152	2421	677	349	1163	1474	547	939	1344	141	844	2050	825	2954	907	2230	2723	3001	706	1272
Kansas City, MO	784	800	1026	1421	961	526	584	489	603	764	732	482		1616	451	1466	565	436	844	1196	184	1246	1127	1246	840	1797	248	1073	1808	1844	1066	198
Key West, FL	2099	809	2646	1659	886	1534	1275	1455	2222	1515	1334	1348	1617	2884	1159	160	1632	1944	1010	1446	1807	387	1357	2514	1332	3417	1370	2693	3386	3464	1213	1735
Las Vegas, NV	572	1959	973	2714	2199	1746	1932	1220	747	2013	1457	1828	1349	270	1581	2525	1786	1656	1739	2518	1278	2303	2480	285	2190	1023	1600	419	569	1128	2428	1164
Lexington, KY	1371	369	1610	917	400	370	83	876	1186	344	996	184	581	2158	423	1030	464	782	745	701	771	817	638	1833	370	2381	334	1657	2392	2428	533	773
Little Rock, AR	877	515	1407	1447	754	650	617	319	965	885	439	583	381	1666	136	1147	724	815	425	1230	574	925	1150	1340	905	2211	345	1488	1963	2275	1015	446
Los Angeles, CA	786	2174	1240	2983	2414	2015	2172	1437	1015	2281	1550	2068	1616		1794	2735	2055	1925	1894	2787	1546	2515	2713	370	2428	963	1821	688	380	1134	2670	1377
Memphis, TN	1008	379	1477	1312	619	531	482	453	1097	742	575	464	451	1794		1012	622	831	394	1094	641	778	1014	1471	768	2245	283	1524	2095	2299	879	577
Mexico City, DF	1404	1718	2301	2768	1962	2017	1979	1090	1756	2254	924	1963	1598	1839	1500	2111	2100	2032	1272	2571	1735	1889	2471	1469	2279	2768	1721	2003	2218	2842	2336	1440
Miami, FL	1952	661	2497	1482	728	1381	1127	1307	2069	1354	1186	1198	1466	2735	1012		1475	1791	861	1288	1658	235	1180	2362	1173	3260	1221	2544	3038	3315	1044	1587
Milwaukee, WI	1354	809	1173	1074	867	90	381	1010	1042	374	1163	272	565	2055	622	1475		337	1015	879	509	1258	849	1817	551	2062	379	1437	2170	1990	788	763
Minneapolis, MN	1225	1127	838	1396	1180	408	703	928	913	696	1171	591	436	1925	831	1791	337		1223	1204	372	1573	1171	1687	874	1727	563	1308	2040	1655	1110	634
Mobile, AL	1234	328	1874	1427	571	917	721	589	1414	978	468	733	802	2014	382	719	1011	1224	144	1202	1038	491	1101	1643	1000	2621	645	1936	2320	2727	965	894
Montréal, QC	2129	1218	2099	310	980	847	824	1722	1832	560	1884	847	1330	2845	1314	1647	938	1262	1640	382	1302	1437	454	2591	603	2948	1092	2228	2960	2916	587	1529
Nashville, TN	1219	248	1586	1099	408	469	273	664	1158	534	786	287	555	2006	209	913	564	881	532	884	747	692	802	1682	560	2357	307	1633	2306	2404	667	688
New Orleans, LA	1165	468	1868	1520	712	923	804	519	1398	1066	348	818	844	1894	394	861	1015	1223		1304	1032	641	1222	1523	1090	2642	675	1920	2252	2716	1087	880
New York, NY	2001	882	2041	216	637	787	637	1548	1775	613	1632	707	1196	2787	1094	1288	879	1204	1304		1245	1089	95	2463	369	2891	954	2170	2902	2858	228	1391
Norfolk, VA	1910	558	2132	569	328	878	605	1350	1758	704	1362	720	1155	2707	898	950	969	1295	1026	370	1335	755	271	2373	425	2962	911	2238	2973	2949	193	1349
Oklahoma City, OK	542	844	1203	1678	1084	792	846	206	631	1029	437	739	348	1326	466	1476	876	788	722	1460	452	1254	1384	1005	1101	1922	496	1200	1627	1948	1344	160
Omaha, NE	863	992	845	1436	1151	470	722	656	534	736	898	613	184	1546	641	1658	509	372	1032	1245		1436	1212	1325	914	1650	439	930	1662	1663	1151	298
Orlando, FL	1730	440	2275	1288	526	1153	905	1086	1851	1144	965	968	1246	2515	778	235	1258	1573	641	1089	1436		986	2145	975	3048	999	2323	2816	3093	849	1365
Ottawa, ON	2039	1158	1768	428	920	760	732	1632	1748	471	1804	757	1240	2763	1230	1618	859	1032	1582	440	1125	1448	447	2501	546	2660	1002	2142	2877	2586	566	1439
Philadelphia, PA	1924	780	2011	306	539	757	571	1467	1732	583	1547	643	1127	2713	1014	1180	849	1171	1222	95	1212	986		2387	305	2861	888	2140	2873	2828	137	1319
Phoenix, AZ	425	1844	1210	2681	2088	1795	1849	1066	908	2032	1178	1742	1246	373	1471	2362	1817	1687	1523	2463	1325	2145	2387		2104	1332	1499	653	749	1414	2348	1053
Pittsburgh, PA	1641	684	1713	570	446	459	288	1221	1447	285	1354	359	840	2428	768	1173	551	874	1090	369	914	975	305	2104		2563	604	1842	2574	2530	243	1035
Portland, ME	2315	1192	2333	107	938	1079	967	1861	2067	825	1940	1034	1518	3082	1408	1585	1176	1492	1616	304	1533	1385	402	2778	666	3186	1279	2461	3196	3151	535	1710
Portland, OR	1363	2603	891	3086	2761	2118	2369	2128	1256	2385	2356	2260	1797	963	2260	3260	2062	1727	2642	2891	1650	3048	2861	1332	2563		2050	765	635	174	2800	1764
Rapid City, SD	843	1508	323	1900	1670	912	1208	1061	397	1200	1291	1100	704	1312	1160	2173	840	575	1551	1708	525	1956	1675	1305	1378	1215	959	649	1384	1142	1618	699
Reno, NV	1019	2396	958	2881	2555	1913	2163	1668	1051	2180	1904	2056	1591	470	2029	3063	1953	1818	2186	2685	1445	2841	2656	733	2357	578	1844	518	218	720	2595	1558
Richmond, VA	1832	532	2051	547	293	797	512	1278	1671	622	1329	627	1069	2620	824	944	888	1210	1002	334	1259	742	245	2294	344	2869	822	2145	2880	2868	108	1261
St. Louis, MO	1037	555	1278	1182	714	295	348	630	854	533	784	243	248	1821	283	1221	379	563	675	954	439	999	888	1499	604	2050		1326	2061	2096	827	442
Salt Lake City, UT	599	1878	552	2365	2037	1398	1647	1403	533	1664	1634	1541	1073	688	1524	2544	1437	1308	1920	2170	930	2323	2140	653	1842	765	1326		735	839	2079	1042
San Antonio, TX	712	986	1480	2039	1230	1202	1210	276	935	1439	195	1149	766	1357	727	1379	1285	1205	541	1822	920	1160	1742	985	1495	2076	906	1311	1736	2150	1607	625
San Diego, CA	810	2138	1302	3046	2381	2080	2196	1359	1077	2346	1472	2089	1597	120	1819	2656	2118	1986	1816	2809	1613	2436	2738	355	2452	1083	1845	750	501	1256	2693	1401
San Francisco, CA	1086	2472	1173	3098	2712	2130	2380	1734	1268	2397	1929	2273	1808	382	2095	3038	2170	2040	2252	2902	1662	2816	2873	749	2574	635	2061	735		807	2812	1775
Santa Fe, NM	58	1379	943	2212	1618	1313	1379	640	391	1562	877	1272	766	846	998	1944	1336	1211	1087	1994	891	1723	1917	520	1634	1388	1029	625	1144	1463	1879	572
Sault Ste. Marie, ON	1777	1040	1273	923	947	483	577	1370	1428	348	1527	540	951	2465	972	1685	400	545	1355	921	850	1475	911	2240	614	2166	740	1848	2581	2090	854	1150
Seattle, WA	1438	2649	818	3054	2808	2063	2363	2193	1320	2353	2431	2253	1844	1134	2299	3315	1990	1655	2716	2858	1663	3093	2828	1414	2530	174	2096	839	807		2768	1828
Spokane, WA	1320	2369	541	2774	2528	1785	2084	1964	1091	2075	2192	1973	1564	1216	2018	3035	1712	1377	2409	2580	1383	2814	2550	1381	2252	352	1817	720	874	279	2490	1600
Tampa, FL	1746	451	2293	1342	578	1166	916	1102	1860	1178	980	984	1225	2759	779	280	1260	1578	651	1138	1445	85	1040	2153	1023	3064	1008	2340	2832	3111	904	1381
Toronto, ON	1800	963	1771	548	756	519	493	1393	1504	231	1551	518	1001	2517	983	1483	609	933	1306	489	1174	1284	497	2262	316	2620	763	1899	2502	2588	486	1188
Tulsa, OK	645	782	1234	1576	1022	687	738	258	692	927	487	635	263	1433	402	1414	773	704	671	1350	380	1192	1282	1107	994	1938	392	1215	1731	2012	1234	175
Vancouver, BC	1575	2785	953	3188	2944	2198	2499	2338	1465	2487	2565	2389	1980	1275	2437	3451	2125	1790	2851	2993	1799	3229	2963	1550	2665	313	2232	973	947	141	2903	1973
Washington, DC	1885	637	1951	439	398	697	512	1332	1671	522	1411	582	1066	2670	879	1044	788	1110	1087	228	1151	849	137	2348	244	2800	827	2079	2812	2768		1258
Wichita, KS	591	955	1064	1613	1092	724	779	361	519	964	595	674	198	1377	577	1587	763	634	880	1391	298	1365	1319	1053	1035	1764	442	1042	1775	1828	1258	

Mileages in this chart are based upon the routes usually followed by motorists. Highway systems include interstate, U.S., and state highways.